Unraveling Reform Rhetoric

Unraveling Reform Rhetoric

What Educators Need to Know and Understand

Jeff Swensson, John Ellis, and Michael Shaffer

ROWMAN & LITTLEFIELD
Lanham • Boulder • New York • London

Published by Rowman & Littlefield
An imprint of The Rowman & Littlefield Publishing Group, Inc.
4501 Forbes Boulevard, Suite 200, Lanham, Maryland 20706
www.rowman.com

6 Tinworth Street, London SE11 5AL

Copyright © 2019 by Jeff Swensson, John Ellis, Michael Shaffer

All rights reserved. No part of this book may be reproduced in any form or by any electronic or mechanical means, including information storage and retrieval systems, without written permission from the publisher, except by a reviewer who may quote passages in a review.

British Library Cataloguing in Publication Information Available

Library of Congress Cataloging-in-Publication Data

Names: Jeff Swensson, John Ellis, Michael Shaffer
Title: Unraveling Reform Rhetoric: What Educators Need to Know and Understand
ISBN: 978-1-4758-5075-8 (cloth)
ISBN: 978-1-4758-5076-5 (paper)
ISBN: 978-1-4758-5077-2 (electronic)

Contents

Preface: Climb Out on a Limb with Us! — vii
Introduction: How This Primer Works — 1

1. The Primary Purpose of Traditional Public Education versus Free Market Theory — 5
2. Primer? Primer? We Don't Need a Stinking Primer! — 9
3. Where in the World Is Traditional Public Education? — 15
4. The Mechanisms Sold as Education in the Free Market — 41
5. Let's Meet Two Advocates for Free Market Schooling — 45
6. The Sinkhole That Is Context of the Free Market — 51
7. Free Market ATMs from Coast to Coast — 67
8. The Public Good and Traditional Public Education — 79
9. What Educators Don't Know about the Free Market Hurts — 97
10. Students Sold Short in the Free Market — 105
11. Subtlety in the Free Market: "Yeah, but…" — 115
12. The Free Market Is a Desperate Place—Traditional Public Education to the Rescue! — 125
13. What It Takes to Climb Off the Limb — 127

References — 133
Index — 141
About the Authors — 143

Preface

Climb Out on a Limb with Us!

When the three of us started our careers, we had no idea that everyone associated with traditional public education would end up out on a limb.

We relish the professional and personal privilege of working with and learning from colleagues, parents/caregivers, stakeholders, and students in traditional public education. Our service throughout the better part of five decades in education encompasses a diverse array of schools and school districts: small towns, urban areas, suburbs, large cities, richly diverse populations, relatively homogeneous student enrollments—all enriched by a broad range of socioeconomic and family circumstances.

Across time and throughout these many locales, traditional public education faced challenges and enjoyed successes. We know that in traditional U.S. public education there is an endless capacity for transformative outcomes, regardless of grade level, subject area, or any demographic factors, throughout our schools. Furthermore, the capacities of our students, our colleagues, and our communities are the lifeblood of the essential link between traditional public education and U.S. democracy.

But while millions of us worked to fulfill the primary purpose and the student-centered outcomes of traditional public education, too few noticed a change for the worse. For the past several decades, the need for, and positive outcomes from, traditional public education were pushed further and further away from the core of our society and from the fulfillment of our democracy. Traditional public school educators, by and large, kept our heads down and persisted on behalf of better futures for our students.

Only a few noteworthy traditional public education colleagues pushed back in an attempt to validate the central importance of traditional public schools (Berliner & Biddle, 1995; Bracey, 2004, 2009; Ravitch, 2013). They suffer the slings and arrows without enough active support from the millions of us who live the virtues, dedication, and hard work of traditional public education. Traditional public education professionals cannot stand idly by when there is a need to create a lasting and broad-based defense of the worth of traditional public education.

The time has come to defend traditional U.S. public education. Our years of working with thousands upon thousands of people demonstrate that all human beings have the capacity and the right to learn how to think. This book serves as a primer that sets the groundwork for traditional public education colleagues to fashion actionable professional behaviors from the resources embedded in our ongoing work.

Jeff Swensson
John Ellis
Michael Shaffer
Spring 2019

Introduction

How This Primer Works

As all educators know, a primer is a text used to introduce a subject. The subject of this primer concerns the state of U.S. traditional public education. This discussion does not introduce traditional public education, of course, but it does introduce the subject of free market theory and how adherents of this theory push traditional public education into an unwarranted and precarious position.

Like every good primer, this discussion is organized to give readers knowledge about a subject that receives too little attention. Making sense of where traditional public education finds itself, and understanding how educators got in this position, are necessary for professional practice and the purpose of traditional public education to get back on solid ground. To this end, several organizational elements in this primer build knowledge for traditional public education colleagues about the forces and factors that push professional practices and the purpose of traditional public education out on a limb.

HOW TO USE THIS PRIMER

"What traditional public educators can do" sections within this discussion provide introductory thoughts about dealing with the forces and factors pushing our professional purpose and practice away from the core of our society. These strategies are meant as recommendations, not recipes. Thus, readers can modify, adapt, and/or extend our recommendations to generate localized data and information about the threat to traditional public education that few colleagues recognize.

TABLES

Tables are shared within the primer. These echo ideas, and reinforce connections between ideas, in this exploration. Tables, further, serve as suggestions about elements of structure in professional practice that colleagues can adapt, adopt, or ignore to craft quality instruction in pursuit of the primary purpose of traditional public education. Finally, tables introduce stipulated constructs with the intent of differentiating traditional public education from the forces and factors pushing against the profession.

ABIDING ASSUMPTIONS

Several abiding assumptions support and guide the discussion shared throughout this book. It is assumed that U.S. democracy requires balance between individual and public goods. It is assumed, further, that meaning-making and natural thinking are persistent human capacities. Further, this discussion is based on the assumption that thinking and learning are complex and best understood when aligned with research-based definitions. Finally, it is assumed that the practice of traditional public education evolves through continuous improvement so that the primary purpose of traditional public education is fulfilled for all students.

WHAT STUDENTS DESERVE

All students deserve learning experiences to grow and extend their meaning-making into the balance between individual freedom and the covenant accessible when individuals know *how to think*. Learning *how to think* is the primary purpose of comprehensive traditional public education.

SNAPSHOTS

Colleagues, stakeholders, and students provide a wealth of insights into the value of traditional public education; so, allegorical snapshots of this impact are included throughout this primer. These are composite representations of impressive people and serve as reminders of the transformative power of our profession.

MODEL-OF AND MODEL-FOR PROFESSIONAL PRACTICE

Traditional public education, and this primer, are composed of *model-of* and *model-for* professional practices necessary for the pursuit of *how to think*, the primary purpose of traditional public education. Model-of practice describes and explains existing professional practice. Model-for practice describe ideas or concepts that might become professional practice.

SHARE AND SHARE ALIKE

Traditional public education colleagues are team players who share ideas, strategies, and resources to craft quality instruction. This primer is designed to fill the knowledge gap that separates traditional public education colleagues from the intrusion of a free market for schooling in the United States. The intent of this book, also, is to foster a collaborative, extensive dialogue among traditional public educators about the knowledge needed to push back against the forces and factors eroding the purpose, quality, and outcomes of traditional public education.

REFERENCES ARE RESOURCES

References from various scholarly sources are cited throughout to encourage colleagues to gather additional information and insight about professional practice that benefits students and that wards off the free market for schooling in America.

WHOSE CUP OF TEA?

Despite the best intentions, this primer will not be every educator's cup of tea. Just as educators value the diversity of our nation and its students, they value the almost endless perspectives about how best to engage children and young people in learning *how to think*.

Adding to the dialogue about the practice of traditional public education while emphasizing that the time has come to defend our profession vigorously is the primary objective of this book. Even if some traditional public education colleagues do not agree with this perspective, or if some of the information is not relevant to their teaching and learning environment, the goal of this discussion is that all professional practice that establishes *how to think* benefits from this intense focus on the need for a more robust defense of traditional public education.

ONE

The Primary Purpose of Traditional Public Education versus Free Market Theory

The primary purpose of traditional public education is to ensure that all students learn *how to think*. Whether directly or indirectly, all professional behaviors and decisions of public education colleagues are committed to this goal. It is the province of traditional public education to establish this capacity across the broad, diverse, and inclusive constituency of America's students. Dedication to this primary purpose of traditional public education is essential to the future of each student and, thus, to the success of U.S. democracy.

John Dewey signified the value of the link between traditional public education and U.S. democracy when he observed that "a society which is mobile, which is full of channels for the distribution of a change occurring anywhere, must see to it that its members are educated to personal initiative and adaptability" (Dewey, 1916, p. 41). A century later, Dewey's insight into the necessity for an American education dedicated to engaging the broad range of capacities in all individuals in service to democracy is no less accurate but is much more in peril.

Anyone affiliated with traditional U.S. public education feels the negative impact of forces and factors seeking to replace the experience of education fundamental to democracy with a free market for schooling. Despite realizing that traditional public education is being pushed out on a limb, too few traditional public educators understand the origins and the outcomes of this assault. Misidentification of the origins of this assault and too few actionable strategies to defend the worth of traditional public education compound the negative impact of free market theory.

HAMBURGERS SOLD, SCHOOLS OPENED, STUDENTS EDUCATED?

Although it is one thing when fast-food restaurants celebrate the number of hamburgers sold, it's another thing entirely when adherents of a free market for schooling are reduced to identifying success in terms of the growth of the number of choice schools (Long, 2018; Lubienski, 2013).

In the process of advertising the number of students enrolled and the number of schools opened, free marketeers ignore data and details endemic to choice schooling: low student achievement, ingrained segregation, and inequality. If it can be said that expanding numbers constitute the success of free market schooling, it also must be said that hidden behind the numbers "it appears that schools in competitive environments are instead arranged into hierarchies based on who is likely to be served" (Lubienski, Gulosino, & Weitzel, 2009, p. 639).

Battered by the free market numbers game, assailed by cascading statutory demands from the state level, and uncertain how to meet our primary purpose while under siege, traditional public educators respond with classroom and schoolwide activities designed to chase the new marketplace rabbit. This chase shapes the misdirection fostered by the free market and its mechanisms, mandates, goals, processes, and contexts.

Colleagues in traditional public education zig-zag, circle, and spin to accommodate the requirements of this misdirection. Programs, tests, textbooks, and/or instructional requirements emerge from the free market like traps and pitfalls in a video game. Misdirections multiply, double down, and/or disappear with little or no correspondence to the primary purpose of traditional public education.

Observers portray this state of affairs unambiguously: "We could hardly have designed a worse system for supporting good teaching had we tried" (Green, E., 2018, p. 10).

INSTEAD OF TALLYING, TEACHING AND LEARNING

Nevertheless, for the vast array of teaching and learning environments that traditional public school colleagues experience each day, there are professional practices and research-based constructs available to improve and advance *how to think* for all students.

Because educators take their profession's ultimate worth from the realization of this primary purpose for all students, a primer is necessary to highlight the obstacles lying in the path of fulfillment of *how to think*. A free market of schooling tallies, mechanizes, and restricts to block outcomes of value; information about this serious threat to quality teaching and learning in the United States is a new subject for too many traditional public educators.

Free market theory and its impact on teaching and learning in the United States deserve attention. As attention to, and funding for, the implementation of free market theory for America's students grow, the quality, impact, and direction of traditional public education is affected negatively. As this happens, the contributions of traditional public education to American democracy atrophy along with the dreams of a significant portion of U.S. citizens.

This discussion relies upon information, concepts, data, research, and strategies to articulate both where traditional public education is and how it got there.

MODEL-OF AND MODEL-FOR

A multitude of routes can be taken and an almost endless variety of research-based resources are available to reach the primary purpose, the end in mind, of traditional public education. Many existing resources and routes—often having a direct impact on the quality of instruction—are woven into existing classroom practice. These options, choices, decisions, and behaviors will be referenced as *model-of* ideas or applications.

Model-of professional behaviors are mature routes that follow existing concepts, strategies, and thinking behaviors into daily instruction to teach habits of mind. This discussion gives examples of these model-of instructional behaviors to illuminate the practices that colleagues already undertake to teach students *how to think*. Model-of instructional behaviors shared in this book are descriptive-of-practice (Bolsen, 2013).

On the other side of the instructional coin, there are any number of rarely used or little known resources and routes, as well as resources and routes validated by new research or newly crafted during colleague responses to learning. These options, choices, decisions, and behaviors will be referred to as *model-for* ideas or applications.

Model-for professional behaviors are evolving and not in general use to engage students with *how to think*. Model-for professional behaviors incorporate concepts, strategies, and thinking behaviors that accelerate or transform existing practice or innovate to establish new knowledge for original professional practice.

Often model-for behaviors arise when traditional public educators invent instruction to fulfill the primary purpose when existing instructional practices fall short. Model-for behaviors, and some of the theories, concepts, and strategies employed to initiate them, are presented throughout this primer as professional perceptions about what could or should be incorporated in the evolving practice of public education.

Model-for professional behaviors and the cognition that supports them reflect Vygotsky's "important notion of a *zone of proximal development*, which refers to functions that have not yet matured but are in the process of maturation" (Sternberg & Grigorenko, 2004, p. 279). Model-for behaviors in the practice of traditional public education are emerging, not yet mature. Thus, model-for behaviors shared in this book are injunctive-of-practice (Bolsen, 2013).

These two categories of professional behavior suggest the nature of the routes and resources colleagues utilize to introduce elements of cognitive interplay to the capacities of each student. Each category provides a means to talk about the composition of professional practices that provide value to traditional public education. These two categories also constitute a shorthand to reference the research, data, and conceptual frameworks pushed further and further out on a limb by free market theory.

Above all, this primer serves as another means by which traditional public educators can sustain and grow quality professional practice. Traditional public education can, should, and will defend itself more effectively against the free market and the intent of its proponents to push traditional public education into free fall. The future of U.S. students and the future of democracy depend on an inclusive, academically rigorous, and socially just traditional public education.

TWO

Primer? Primer? We Don't Need a Stinking Primer!

Actually, traditional public education colleagues need a primer desperately. Although traditional public educators know the positive impact of quality professional practices, a lack of knowledge about the effect of, and obstacles within, free market theory interfere with outcomes that America's students deserve. A primer, then, is required to end the detrimental influence of free market theory and bring traditional public education away from its current, precarious, perch.

A primer is necessary for several reasons. First, this discussion introduces the free market as a merry-go-round of mechanisms, catch-as-catch-can school types, and funding. What's up and what's down for proponents of schooling aligned with the free market does not depend on the quality of teaching and learning but on contexts designed to serve the needs of entrepreneurs, policy-makers, politicians, and ideologues.

Next, this primer is necessary because it shares data that demonstrates that the free market for schooling is limited and limiting. Return on investment (ROI), instead of Return to Students (RTS), abounds in the free market. Returns from free market schooling cost students, families, citizens, and society.

In addition, a primer is necessary because although proponents proclaim that a free market liberates consumers, the unhappy outcome in the market for U.S. students is that they are subject to the teaching and learning vagaries of choice schooling or privatization without recourse to a present or future endowed with cognitive agency (Lubienski, Gulosino, & Weitzel, 2009). U.S. students are trapped by schooling whose advocates cannot see and do not admit market failure.

CAVEAT EMPTOR: MARKET FAILURE

A paradox lies at the heart of the challenge to purpose and quality for teaching and learning in the United States: the free market and its self-proclaimed successes are harbingers of market failure. Devoted to installing mechanisms (e.g., vouchers, charter schools, tax credits) instead of student achievement, social justice, or balance, free market schooling (often referenced as choice schooling or privatization) abandons the ostensible purposes of education: leading to *how to think* capable of balance between individual and public goods. Buyers must beware; market failure happens once choice mechanisms operate.

Introducing the impact of the free market for schooling provides information necessary for traditional public educators to begin to climb down and return to solid ground.

- When marketplace adherents envision choice schooling as a greater good, this ideological looking glass brings into focus the goal of marketplace competition between entities, schools, and management companies in pursuit of enhanced profit (Lubienski, Gulosino, & Weitzel, 2009, p. 624).

  "Missing in the ideological embrace of choice for choice's sake is any suggestion of the public school as a public good—as a centering locus for a community and as a shared pillar of the commonweal, in which all citizens have an investment" (Mead, 2016).

  In short, one future that exists in the minds of choice proponents is schooling as nothing more than an array of disconnected profit centers. The market fails students and families but provides marketeers with exactly what they want. Market failure for everyone but marketeers is a constant feature of free market schooling but is of no consequence to proponents of free market theory.

- From the perspective of its adherents, the marketplace is supposed to offer multiple, unconstrained choices of efficient schooling for all consumers. But, choice in the U.S. educational marketplace is manipulated—constrained by profit seeking, restrictive enrollment standards, hidden fees, and other more malevolent factors.

  As Calsamiglia, Haeringer, and Klijn (2010) discovered, mechanisms of school choice (vouchers, charter schools, tax credits, etc.) limit or constrain the number and availability of marketplace schools. Market failure is created by this state of affairs because "the introduction of the constraint is also shown to reduce efficiency and stability and to increase segregation" (Calsamiglia, Haeringer, & Klijn, 2010, p. 1873).

  While marketplace proponents contend that families, students, and caregivers benefit from the opportunity to choose schools using the mechanisms of privatization, the fact of the matter is that

what is "free" about the market is that it freely constrains, curtails, controls, and/or confounds free choice in service to the agenda of free market theory.
- Advocates of the marketplace believe that efficiency results from privatization and denotes, unto itself, the success of marketplace schooling. Efficiency is defined as the culling of inefficient schools when these schools are abandoned by parents and caregivers with the result that fiscal support supplied by mechanisms is withdrawn.

  This fiscal support reverts to supposedly efficient schools, which are defined as schools selected by parents and caregivers after leaving the school they first selected. Not only is efficiency defined in terms that have little to do with academic achievement, personal improvement, or thinking skills, but the mechanisms supplying dollars for stealth-schooling entail costs that are anything but efficient.

  As Abdulkadiroglu, Pathak, and Walters (2015) discovered, once dollars are available via choice mechanisms, true efficiency evaporates because low-quality schools set up shop quickly, offer low-level learning to students, scoop up profit, and resist closing. And, as Lubienski et al. (2009) indicate, "research on the underlying assumptions of competitive incentives raises significant issues regarding how these incentives actually play out in the real world of schooling" (p. 611).

  Wong and Shen (2006, p. 1) suggest that school choice is so complicated that competing institutions, political expediency, disparate policies, institutional decisions, and ideological myopia operate at cross purposes and deconstruct any marketplace imagined for U.S. education.

  In the long run, efficiency is little more than a grand supposition of marketplace advocates; the inefficiencies inherent in this delusion embody market failure, a cost that marketeers do not acknowledge.
- Marketplace mavens assume that private sector characteristics, including investor demand, personal consequences for success or failure, and the virtues of competition, "drive executives to press on productivity and the bottom line" (Hess, 2010, p. 45).

  Failure is built into this assumption about free markets of U.S. schooling because the imposition of productivity (a private sector construct of value when building cars or motherboards) short circuits the outcome that parents and caregivers most care about: their child's learning and well-being.

  Market failure occurs when productivity is anchored to mechanisms, the context of free market schooling, and not to the cognitive outcomes associated with quality instruction devoted to *how to*

think for all students. Marketplace adherents, at the end of the day, espouse the value of schooling in marketplace competition that benefits only those who can afford to buy in.
- Marketplace descriptors and expectations superimpose constructs irrelevant to traditional public education and to the relationship of traditional public education with democracy.

    The market's disavowal of the responsibility of education to improve thinking, expand social engagement, and maximize social justice in a democracy demonstrates a salient failure: the marketplace is amoral (Lubienski, 2013). The imposition of mechanisms and the presumptions of value from this context—both of which are disconnected from the cognitive, economic, and social needs of the young citizens of American democracy—deliver market failure to students and our society.

    If privatization and the free market rely on amorality to shield choice schooling from responsibility for the future of all students and the vitality of U.S. democracy, then distress about this ideology is multiplied: privatization fails because it succeeds only on its own terms.
- The educational marketplace, as Ringold (2005) illustrates, does a remarkably poor job of informing all parents/caregivers and students about the availability of choice schools.

    The market is subject to manipulation of information with the result that families and students of poverty or color frequently are left out of the loop when it comes to knowledge about school choice (Fleming, Cowen, Witte, & Wolf, 2013). As a result, these consumers are subjected to the failure of the market because the nature of the market and its mechanisms takes away the ability to maximize individual advantage or preferences.

    Privatization fails to offer the advantages of a market to all "consumers" (otherwise known as parents and caregivers) because privatization proponents envision and espouse a market for stealth-schooling that is vendor-centric. Where vendors don't perceive that a profit can be made, vendors are unlikely to set up shop. Marketplace schooling purveyors tend to locate in proximity to consumers able to bankroll their business.
- The marketplace depends upon a laissez-faire regulatory environment both among different states and within individual states (Wong & Shen, 2006).

    Free market expectations—of the kind promulgated through the influence of well-connected and well-heeled marketeers who acquiesce to the amorality necessary in markets—open the door to acquisitive practices of choice schools, school management corporations, and businesses with a fiduciary interest in profit from school choice (Figlio & Hart, 2010; Zernike, 2016).

The profit motive and self-aggrandizing behaviors of marketeers illuminate the self-aggrandizing essence of my-side bias (Molden & Higgins, 2012) prevalent when market success is based on advantages that accrue to the proponents in charge of the market. Devoted to the success of the market itself and its adherents, privatization proffers *consumer failure* to cohorts of our society that do not fit the vendor-centric, profit-producing, ideology-enhancing agenda written into implementation of the free market.

- Ultimately, market failure is in the hands of marketplace ideologues who eschew an emphasis on providing excellence in achievement (teaching and learning) to assert a greater value in the imposition of theoretical purity through policy.

The question arises even among ideologues, however, to what educational end or outcome can this purity be directed (Hess, 2010). Marketplace adherents admit that "simply legislating 'school choice' programs, or enrolling a child in a charter school, will have no obvious short-term impact on achievement" (Hess, 2010, p. 41). Undeterred by such rare bursts of insightful self-reflection, privatization proponents maintain a laser-like focus on ideology.

Although ideologues attempt to compensate with hyperbole, myth, and mechanisms for the desultory impact of marketplace schooling on student learning and well-being, nothing reverses the dedication of the free market to self-perpetuation. Having concocted numerous fairy tales, privatization proponents are only too interested in asserting that marketplace schooling is the fairest schooling of them all.

- Context puts school choice advocates in the same failed conceptual realm as those critics of public education who, at one point in the history of American education, proposed teacher-proof curriculum (Berry, Johnson, & Montgomery, 2005).

Ignoring education as a people business, marketplace adherents imagine that context—its mechanisms—suffices to leaven the uncertainty, creativity, flexibility, thinking, and unstructured nature of human beings. As scholars observe accurately, American education does not constitute "the pure markets idealized by some thinkers" (Lubienski, Gulosino, & Weitzel, 2009, p. 605).

Adherents of a free market have no need to orient professional practice on the road to *how to think* and no need to acknowledge the evolution of a mosaic of professional practices to inspire the growth and improvement of student cognition. Instead, the market restrains and confines while proclaiming freedom and reform.

CHEAP GOODS AND FALSE PROMISES

The false promises and cheap goods (mechanisms, context, competition, and choice) sold in the free market burden students, families, communities, and the nation with thinking-as-rejection, amorality, and stealth-schooling. Deliberate avoidance of function and successful intelligence gives privatization adherents the ability to hide behind lukewarm statements about quality where substance evaporates into suppositions and images of what stealth-schooling "might be" and "may be" (Loeb, Valant, & Kasman, 2011, pp. 145–146).

The marketplace—mirages, sleight of hand, bait and switch, and shell games—echoes with a carnival barker's call from ideologues to the detriment of U.S. students who deserve traditional public education where the conditions necessary and sufficient for all students in all schools to learn lie at the center of a primary purpose.

In the meantime, privatization (for-profit charter and private schools that accept vouchers) and commercialization (sales of standardized tests, curricula, and management services) grow profit for marketeers while, simultaneously, public funding expands to support the full range of choice education from for-profit to parochial schools (Boesenberg, 2003).

THREE

Where in the World Is Traditional Public Education?

Out on a limb. Traditional public education in the United States is out on a limb and this is not where students and the country need educators to be. Nevertheless, despite the dedicated, compassionate, and thought-filled efforts of millions of colleagues in traditional public education, the profession is stranded.

Realizing where traditional public education is, and how it got in this position, begins with an understanding of the value-added potential of the effective practices in traditional public education. These are first steps on a journey to refocus, reorient, and improve the place of traditional public education in the evolving nature of American society.

Realizing both the model of and model for professional behaviors necessary for the futures of students in the twenty-first century requires establishing conceptual benchmarks for professional practice in traditional public education. This chapter shares an amalgam of these behaviors that is critical to understanding the profession of traditional public education.

Climbing Down from a Precarious Position

In this chapter, the combination of the teaching and learning quality illustrates what must be established from this beginning. Ultimately, this beginning will allow traditional public educators to defend the purpose and quality of teaching and learning that all U.S. students deserve.

TEACHER SNAPSHOT: MR. HOUSTON

Innumerable public education colleagues dedicate themselves to engaging students in learning how to think with the verve embodied in the professionalism of our colleague Jeremy Houston. A musician in his own right, "Major Houston," as the students called him affectionately, lived the hard work, beauty, and emotion of music in his instruction as the leader of an incredibly diverse, large, high school band.

Jeremy Houston did not emphasize winning any of the multitude of band competitions his ensemble entered during the school year. Instead, he taught students to learn-into the highest level of thinking at the core of their individual playing on behalf of the entire band. To grow and improve one note, one measure, one class, one rehearsal, one student's thinking at a time was the demand Mr. Houston made of himself during every interaction with his students.

As a lab class, band involved the application of a complex assortment of expectations for thinking into expected behaviors and actions. Students learned as they were asked to call forward previous knowledge, as they worked to compare and contrast different tempos for segments of a piece of music, or as they evaluated the degree of improvement of their own playing.

For Major Houston, the success of his teaching lay not in the frequent trophies earned at band competitions. Rather, he judged learning as his success and learning was measured in the improved quality of the thinking that the band demonstrated every time they played.

It was amazing how many different opportunities Mr. Houston created for his students to demonstrate improvement. The band, the sections of the band, individual players in the band: all played and re-played different portions of any given piece of music.

Major Houston's classroom command of varied instructional tools during every class gave band students opportunities to develop and use knowledge and skills to create new meaning, new learned cognition and behavior. All this growth in learning over time occurred when mistakes, miscues, sour notes, and missed downbeats were transformed by a teacher dedicated to engaging students in how to think.

"Well," the major would say when a learning outcome had not been reached, "no worries, you just haven't learned that, yet." The signal, the lesson, in the three-letter word yet *is that the learner has the capacity to get to a next, higher, level of thinking on behalf of a greater good. The message is that the outcome is in reach and that "not yet" can be transformed. The motivation to learn was inspired by this simple word and the thinking it motivated.*

The successful intelligence—an interplay of cognitive skills to express a complex learning objective—demonstrated by a large multi-aged group of diverse learners that developed when Jeremy Houston orchestrated his vast array of instructional tools constitutes one example of the meaning-making, thinking, learning, and responsive cognition that public education embraces.

Colleagues like Mr. Houston whose day-to-day instruction conveys the excellence of existing practice draw this book into a search for a deeper understanding of theory-into-practice. The goal in this chapter is to share constructs, propositions, and theories that anchor ideas and recommendations about the aspirations that best serve students in traditional public education.

LISTENING TO THAT COLLEAGUE: THEORY INTO PRACTICE

Educators all know at least one colleague who can't resist getting everyone involved in discussions about the theory and concepts at the foundation of quality instructional strategies. During grade level meetings, drinking a cup of coffee together before school, scribbling notes during faculty meetings—theoretically minded colleagues always connect the backstory, the big ideas, as colleagues put together lessons, units, or projects for students. Many times, despite the boundless enthusiasm of THAT colleague, the practical considerations about teaching outweigh paying strict attention to the details of theoretical discourse.

The let's-get-on-with-it focus on the practical side of teaching and learning does not mean, however, that it's right to ignore this colleague's insights. THAT colleague correctly links practical professional thinking to theoretical foundations. After all, understanding and applying the theories and concepts at the heart of professional behaviors make teaching activities more effective.

And, more effective means more meaningful for students. Because improving the cognitive capacities of each student is the persistent, practical, day-to-day goal of the journey toward *how to think* in traditional public education, the theoretical base that supports this approach to teaching and learning gives educators a handle on why they need to articulate the primary purpose of education and how best to reach this end in mind.

Coffee, Tea, Soda, and Theory

It's important to emphasize that this background discussion does do not grind an axe for any one theory or another. By no means are the theories and concepts included in this chapter the only way to engage in quality professional practice. Rather, the ideas in this chapter, and the way they are incorporated throughout this primer, illustrate constructs, theories, and professional practices that traditional public educators may utilize, adapt, or extend to secure implementation of the primary purpose of traditional public education. These thoughts also serve as models-for that any colleague can adapt and apply.

The theoretical frameworks proposed here orient professional thinking about instruction before and during teaching. We know THAT colleague suggested, explained, and discussed a huge number of concepts and ideas but, just as important, THAT colleague gives colleagues a very clear sense of the role of conceptual frameworks for organizing quality instruction.

The frameworks presented here are referred to as *points of practice*. Points of practice engage traditional public educators in the interactive researching, planning, implementing, and evaluating that orient professional practice during the classroom journey to *how to think*.

Traditional public educators should grab a cup of coffee or a soda, when time permits, and read this chapter in conjunction with the vast knowledge base that helps to construct day-to-day instructional choices. Comparing and contrasting allows the application of ideas, strategies, and theories presented here in an amalgam of professional practice that best fits the decisions and cognitive behaviors necessary to engage students with *how to think* in any U.S. classroom.

Just as THAT colleague indicates, when professional practices arise from intentional research-based responses to learning within the exercise of the moral purpose of traditional public education, the impact on the capacities of students is maximized.

PROFESSIONAL PRACTICE IN TRADITIONAL PUBLIC EDUCATION

No apology is given for the intensity of the focus on realizations that arise from professional experiences in traditional public education. Primary among these is the realization that traditional public education is a practice, a work in progress. Traditional public education colleagues embrace continuous improvement to nurture the public good while promoting individual well-being. Therefore, the practice of traditional public education cannot be a linear phenomenon.

As is the case with other professions, the practice of education requires persistent researching, learning, attempting, evaluating, applying, and more learning. This professional feedback loop leads to additional next-steps, iterations of reflecting, researching, learning, attempting, applying, evaluating, and refining to craft a loop for continuous improvement on the professional journey necessary and sufficient to reach the end in mind of traditional public education.

The end in mind for traditional public education is *how to think*. Whether directly or indirectly, professional practices and the decisions made on behalf of students in traditional public education drive toward *how to think*. To be clear, this cognitive destination and primary purpose is 180 degrees away from a destination known as *what* to think. To further clarify, *how to think* is an evolving, difficult-to-reach, and long-range end in mind for every student. *How to think* lies at the core of every substantive interaction in traditional public education.

Two Metaphors for Quality Professional Practice

Two metaphors help explain how concepts become practical—(1) the unique artistry of mosaics and (2) a unique educator's version of a GPS. Each metaphor helps explain the admixture of art and science required to engage all students in traditional public education with *how to think*.

These metaphors are a reminder that very few of the innumerable goals, objectives, and expectations associated with the primary purpose of traditional U.S. public education are realized by following prepackaged recipes or regimented, unchanging, sequences of steps. Likewise, learning is complex human behavior, not a lock-step equation. To create the teaching and learning conditions necessary for the journey to *how to think*, conceptual frameworks that orient and support day-to-day professional decisions and cognitive behaviors are essential.

The Mosaics of Educational Practice

The mosaics metaphor conveys the understanding that professional practice, like that of a mosaics artist, envisions an end in mind and uses a multitude of materials and talents to bring this purpose to life (Dunbar, 2018).

Just as a mosaics artist shapes materials and responds to the developing work at hand, traditional public educators respond with compassion, intellect, creativity, and professionalism to the array of cognitive and developmental interactions in class that signal learning that "can take place in any order at any level, depending on the educational objective, instruction and assessment" (Seaman, 2011, p. 34).

Professional practice is an ever-developing mosaic. Composed of an evolving, always-growing array of behaviors, the intersection of art and science in professional practice also envisions *how to think* as a mosaic of cognition within professional practice and in the learning of each student. Using mosaics as a metaphor conveys the need to identify, repurpose, bring forward, uncover, and illustrate a multitude of behaviors that represent quality professional practice in traditional public education.

Taking advantage of the complexity of human beings, their brains, and their institutions, this primer models how practice in traditional public education is function in perpetual motion. Different pieces of the mosaic of teaching and learning must always be at the ready to orient planning and thinking during responsive professional practice. Both metaphors help recognize the necessity for monitoring and adjusting while responding to learning while on the road to *how to think*.

The GPPS of Professional Practice

Someone once said that the process, "getting there," is half the fun of any journey. There's some truth to this especially if there are ways to orient the choices made and directions taken as the journey unfolds. Nothing is wrong with maps or guideposts, of course, but the best guide for getting there on the journey to *how to think* is a GPPS (Guided Professional Practice Selections).

The point of stipulating this "take" on a GPS is to suggest how colleagues can operationalize the resources and routes that orient the choices, decisions, and applications for quality instruction necessary to reach the primary purpose of traditional public education. The GPPS shared here, for example, is a model-for orienting professional practices and quality education that any colleague can create. The decision-making required for quality instructional practices is oriented by a GPPS.

The model-for GPPS shared here is constructed of six *points of practice*. Constructed from research-based and data-driven studies, these six points of practice require colleagues to identify and select *habits of mind* that inform teaching and learning throughout a school year.

HABITS OF MIND: VERBS OF VALUE

Habits of mind—often referenced as thinking skills—can be relatively simple or very complex. Habits of mind festoon the literature in such profusion that it's not possible to list them all, and teaching them all is not recommended. However, the selection of relevant habits of mind is a cognitive behavior of traditional public educators that is necessary prior to, and during, instruction and learning.

Colleagues and scholars tend to label the complex cognitive behaviors and interconnections among habits of mind with commonly understood terms such as *reasoning, judgment, decision-making,* and *problem-solving.* These labels symbolize the ongoing juxtaposition and interplay of cognitive behaviors when individuals develop and express their capacity for *how to think* (Holyoak & Morrison, 2005).

How to think is fostered by the admixture of the practices of traditional public education with the brain's capacity to establish new knowledge. Habits of mind, cognitive behaviors, are built during day-to-day instruction.

The cognition represented in a habit of mind is described in verbs or verb phrases. Invoking habits of mind echoes Benjamin Bloom's thinking that the descriptive verbs and verb phrases (and nouns employed in the original Taxonomy) denoting habits of mind constitute a "'common language about learning goals to facilitate communication across persons, subject matter, and grade levels'" (Krathwohl, 2002, p. 212).

There is a penchant for, and value to, categorizing thinking skills to facilitate classroom application of this common language. Factor analysis devoted to an examination of the hierarchical nature of Bloom's Original Taxonomy—six categories of thinking skills (Bloom, 1956)—identified *concrete intelligence* and *applied intelligence* as labels to divide the six. Often, concrete intelligence is recognized as an array of lower-order thinking skills while applied intelligence is referred to by an array of higher-order thinking skills.

These two groups of thinking skills are composed of either "lower order (knowledge, comprehension, application) or higher order (analysis, synthesis, evaluation) thinking skills" (Seaman, 2011, p. 34). Organizing, prioritizing, and applying habits of mind are investments by traditional public educators in intelligence fostered by the capacity of all students to learn.

The common language expressed in Bloom's Taxonomy and in habits of mind is understood "'to be a classification of the student behaviors which represent the intended outcomes of the educational process' (Bloom, 1956, p. 12)" (Seaman, 2011, p. 33). Habits of mind are also resources that teach and activate the rich cognitive interplay present alongside and throughout human development of each learner.

Habits of Mind: An Overview

As shared by different scholars and as a descriptive shorthand, habits of mind represent the imperatives for learning outcomes and the possibilities for instruction among which colleagues must choose so that teaching and learning behaviors follow a route toward *how to think*. A small sample, an overview, of these imperatives includes:

- "situated problem solving, observing, classifying, organizing, informal theory building, and testing" (Ritchart & Perkins, 2005, p. 775);
- making connections, asking questions while researching, inferring, prioritizing, activating *a priori* or background knowledge, speculating, identifying what is not part of resource, problem, or perspective (Fisher & Frey, 2008, p. 60);
- recognizing, recalling, explaining, executing, implementing, differentiating, organizing, attributing, checking, critiquing, generating, planning, producing (Krathwohl, 2002, p. 215);
- recognizing cause-effect relationships, making analogies and generalizations, critically examining evidence, using imagination to build narratives (Mezirow, 1997);
- critically examining evidence in a text, seeing the world from several different points of view, connecting ideas and/or finding patterns among ideas, imagining alternatives and possibilities, and deter-

mining the relevance of ideas, data, and points of view (Schmoker, 2006, p. 58); and
- sequencing, comparing, categorizing, drawing inferences, making analogies, considering multiple points of view, dealing with complex information, summarizing, clarifying, predicting, and question generating (Ritchart & Perkins, 2005, pp. 778–789).

Professional practice in traditional public education engages students with the ongoing discovery of new knowledge and new cognitive process. Habits of mind are immersed in this discovery. Professional practice is the pursuit of *how to think* and it engages each student's capability found in multilayered systems of cognition (buttressed by prior experiences, personal assets, and individual emotions). The capability of all students, in response to internal and/or external interactions of professional practice, can yield outcomes (often expressed in behaviors) that are transformative (Thorsen, Gustafsson, & Cliffordson, 2014).

Habits of mind, these verbs of value, are the heart of the resources represented in model-of and model-for instructional behaviors. The priority, at the moment, is to introduce six points of practice. These constitute the GPPS modeled in this book and orient the cognition involved in options, choices, decisions, and applications of professional practice on the journey to *how to think* in the classroom.

AN INTRODUCTION: SIX POINTS OF PRACTICE

The first points of practice are *meaning-making* and *natural thinking*. These two orient professional practice to the capacities and assets that students bring to class. Meaning-making and natural thinking put colleagues in position to understand the value of, and engage the contextual, cultural, and experiential assets of, each student.

The next two points of practice, a *definition of thinking* and a *definition of learning*, orient professional practice that leads out to the maturation and developmental staging of natural thinking and meaning-making. A definition of thinking and a definition of learning guide teaching decisions in relationship to the individual assets and capacities of students.

Making sense of the responses and cognitive behaviors of students is enhanced when it's possible to calibrate teaching and learning progress based on adopted definitions. Definitions of thinking and learning give educators the capacity to acquire and assess feedback from students' cognition. This feedback about the growth of student cognition in relationship to elements in these adopted definitions means it's possible to monitor and adjust cognitive behaviors during professional practice.

Rounding out the half-dozen points of practice in this GPPS are two elements that help make decisions about improving the breadth and depth of instruction in relationship to human development. These last points of practice—*responsive cognition* and *cognitive agency*—orient educators to the relationship between habits of mind and cognitive behaviors via the actions and expressions of each student's cognitive growth during instruction, during active learning, during formative classroom testing, and during projects or activities undertaken beyond the classroom.

Professional Practice Is Not about Perfection

Everyone knows from using a GPS while driving that there are bumps in the road during any journey and there are times when its necessary to "reconfigure" to reach a destination. The difficult work that goes into professional practice and the reconfiguring that is a part of professional practice are facilitated by a GPPS.

Orienting/reconfiguring professional practice and responding to student learning provides traditional public educators with every chance for teaching success because, as Wong (nd) observes, "each person has unlimited potential. Humans are the only species able to improve the quality of their lives." All in all, the points of practice that power a GPPS access the unlimited potential of all learners.

A GPPS GETS EDUCATORS WHERE THEY NEED TO GO

Points of practice facilitate the application of theories and instructional strategies and orient the planning, implementing, and evaluating of teaching and learning along cognitive highways and byways in route to *how to think*. Six points of practice comprise the GPPS that orients professional practice as discussed throughout this book: (1) natural thinking; (2) meaning-making; (3) definitions of thinking; (4) definitions of learning; (5) responsive cognition; and (6) cognitive agency.

At the foundation of these points of practice are, first, the cognitive dimension of both Bloom's Original and Revised Taxonomies (Bloom, 1956; Krathwohl, 2002) and, second, the knowledge dimension in the revised version of Bloom's Taxonomy (Krathwohl, 2002; Seaman, 2011). The confluence of these dimensions and points of practice is shown in Table 3.1.

Elaborating a GPPS

Bloom's Taxonomy and its revision help organize this approach to the use of a GPPS via the dimensions of knowledge and cognitive process. The revision of Bloom's Taxonomy (Krathwohl, 2002) posits four kinds of knowledge (*factual, conceptual, procedural, metacognitive*) and six cognitive processes (*remember, understand, apply, analyze, evaluate, create*) (p. 216). All

Cognitive Process Dimension (K/b) / Knowledge Dimension (K)	REMEMBER (knowledge)	UNDERSTAND (comprehension)	APPLY (application)	ANALYZE (analysis)	EVALUATE (synthesis)	CREATE (evaluation)
FACTUAL Knowledge	Natural thinking (PoP)					
FACTUAL AND CONCEPTUAL Knowledge		Meaning-making (PoP)				
CONCEPTUAL AND PROCEDURAL Knowledge			Definition of thinking, AND definition of learning (PoP)	Definition of thinking, AND definition of learning (PoP)		
PROCEDURAL AND METACOGNITIVE Knowledge					Responsive cognition (PoP)	
METACOGNITIVE Knowledge						Cognitive agency, successful intelligence, AND wisdom (PoP)

Figure 3.1. Points of Practice with Dimensions of Bloom's and Revised Bloom's Taxonomy Adapted from Krathwohl (2002). (Key: b = Bloom; K = Krathwohl; PoP = Points of Practice).

six points of practice incorporate cognitive processes and knowledge in the interplay of habits of mind.

This interplay occurs in conjunction with human development to yield the cognitive agency and successful intelligence necessary and sufficient to craft balance between individual and public goods. Part of the value of points of practice is that they serve as guides that provide essential cues about the confluence of art and science in the function of professional practice.

Seaman's (2011) observation about the revision of Bloom's Taxonomy sets the proper tone for professional practice and is best applied to the application of points of practice in that there is "some overlap between categories so that an emphasis is placed on teacher use as opposed to the development of a strict hierarchy" (p. 37).

Knowledge and Cognitive Process

An interplay of dimensions—knowledge with cognitive process—illuminates a fundamental cognitive characteristic of *how to think*. This characteristic is the brain's ability to weave knowledge and habits of mind through cognitive process via multiple layers of brain function. This ability gives traditional public educators every reason to embrace the perspective shared by Fox and Alexander (2011), who position thinking "as a behavior (Russell, 1961) rather than a skill set or ensemble of processes" (p. 7).

Understanding thinking in this way recalls the insight that habits of mind are cognitive behaviors taught through lessons and, thus, "the active cognitive behaviors that are desired from a student" (Seaman, 2011, p. 36).

The integration of these behaviors within quality instruction is facilitated when an understanding of function in traditional public education is expressed, in part, within and among the intersections of knowledge, cognition, and instruction. A brief discussion of each point of practice allows us to explore further the nature of both quality instruction and function in traditional public education.

Natural Thinking: Point of Practice

Thinking, at its foundation, is an automatic cognitive response to daily living based on individual perceptions of ideas, interactions, and situations that arise (Ritchart & Perkins, 2005). Human beings naturally classify and organize. Natural thinking is an asset students bring to educators every day. As a point of practice, natural thinking orients colleagues to teaching habits of mind that align with *remember* and *recall* from the revision of Bloom's Taxonomy (Krathwohl, 2002).

This first point of practice also establishes the practical value of engaging students with cognitive behaviors that call forth knowledge from students' long-term memory. The importance of this point of practice is recognized by scholars who often describe it as *accessing prior knowledge* (Brown, Roediger, & McDaniel, 2014). Thinking behaviors that gather knowledge from long-term memory are relevant to learning assignments, tasks, questions, and unknowns explored in class (Brown, Roediger, & McDaniel, 2014; Krathwohl, 2002).

Meanwhile, Back in Class (I)

A return visit to Mr. Houston's band class recognizes that his lesson began with recall. *"Ok, take a look at number 36 on your score and take the tune seven measures out. Where have we seen this before?"* Student responses and discussion in relation to Mr. Houston's question recalled various details about a previous piece of music. *"Yes,"* confirmed Mr. Houston. *"Now, how did that previous piece sound?"*

The students sang, da-da-da, the tune from the previous piece. *"Take a look, again, starting at 36; how should THIS sound?"* Recall and remember gave students a cognitive and performance entry point, prior knowledge, for the new knowledge that emerged during the lesson via a new piece of music.

A veteran traditional public educator, Mr. Houston's accessing prior knowledge—a model-of instructional choice—illustrates just one possible route and one possible resource available to engage students in a goal amidst an overall lesson. This choice, like all the others along the instructional journey to *how to think*, is a reminder that points of practice, dimensions in Bloom's Revised Taxonomy, and stages of human development must be accessed as active elements in quality instruction.

Meaning-Making: Point of Practice

Every student walks into every classroom making meaning. Meaning-making is "a developmental measure of how individuals organize their experience, which evolves over time" (Ignelzi, 2000, p. 10). This paraphrase shares Robert Kegan's (1980) theory of meaning-making, which is helpful when educators think about students' cognitive capacities and when educators think about what can be done to design and carry out lessons that grow these capacities.

Based on Kegan's theory, meaning-making occurs along a six-stage continuum: *incorporative, impulsive, imperial, interpersonal, institutional,* and *inter-individual*. This continuum is based on development of an individual's meaning making in relation to others.

This is helpful to know and apply because students' natural thinking and meaning-making are forged, in part, by the developmental maturity of meaning made through individual growth from an inward and insular point of view to an outward and expansive point of view in relation to "the other." The labels of Kegan's continuum signify the expansion of an individual's development in relation to others from earliest—*incorporative*—to most mature—*inter-individual* (Kegan, 1980).

These interactive and sequenced developmental stages are resources for professional practice because they constitute perspectives embedded in how "individuals actively construct their own sense of reality" (Ignelzi, 2000, p. 7). Although many other resources for public education colleagues are often in short supply, teachers can depend upon human beings evolving their own realities as a means by which to orient quality instruction (Ignelzi, 2000).

The value of Kegan's theory of meaning-making for professional practice is that it shines a light on the conjunction of instruction with the developmental capacities and lived experience of individuals as ways to make sense of how students engage with classroom learning. This theory provides an understanding of "the internal structure individuals use to organize meaning-making, and therefore the self, change and evolve in regular and systematic ways" (Ignelzi, 2000, p. 7). In other words, educators are always making sense of things and *this* meaning-making grows and changes developmentally with time and experience.

Kegan puts it this way, "*Human* being is *meaning making*. For the human, what *evolving* amounts to is the *evolving of systems of meaning*; the business of organisms is to organize, as Perry (1970) says" (italics original) (Kegan, 1980, p. 374). Aligning choices about instruction with stages of development evidenced by students allows traditional public education colleagues to lead students out of natural thinking and meaning-making.

Thinking about professional practice, then, means that quality instruction develops habits of mind as cognitive resources for students that can interplay within and among developmental stages illuminated in the scholarship of Kegan (1980) and alongside that of Piaget (1952) and Kohlberg and Hersh (1977).

As an example (based on an understanding of where students begin a school year, cognitively speaking), an educator might teach habits of mind to engage students beyond natural thinking and meaning-making that Kegan would label incorporative, impulsive, or imperial. Leading students out of cognition stalled in factual knowledge and cognitive processing as remember/recall and/or understand is facilitated further when teachers understand how thinking develops into the stages illuminated by the first three of Piaget's cognitive operations: *sensorimotor, pre-operational,* and *concrete operational*. (Kegan, 1980, p. 377; Piaget, 1952).

From the vantage point of Kohlberg's stages of moral development, this start-of-the-year teaching would craft lessons that engage students with the interplay of habits of mind that grow learning out of orientations including *punishment and reward, instrumental,* and *interpersonal concordance* (Kohlberg & Hersh, 1977).

Congruence between the revision of Bloom's Taxonomy, points of practice, and developmental stages conceived by Kegan, Piaget, and Kohlberg enhances an understanding of the maturation of each student's cognitive behaviors in relationship to instruction is shown in Table 3.2. Professional practice becomes more effective, then, when educators engage students with selected habits of mind through the process of meaning-making and developmental stages during the classroom journey toward *how to think* and in synch with the cognitive capacity and other assets that students possess (Kegan, 1980; Krathwohl, 2002).

Traditional education colleagues have the responsibility to implement professional practices that engage students in learning experiences that segue habits of mind with students' knowledge, cognitive process, and developmental stages. This means that student capacity to make meaning is an ever-present resource available to intentional professional practice that nurtures habits of mind.

Understanding that students are always meaning-making amidst developmental stages confirms the value of the primary purpose of education. The practice of traditional public education is an investment in human development so that all students are, to recall Vygotsky's idea, ma-

Cognitive Process Dimension (b/K) / Knowledge Dimension (K)	REMEMBER (Knowledge) incorporative/ke	UNDERSTAND (Comprehension) impulsive/ke	APPLY (Application) imperial/ke	ANALYZE (Analysis) interpersonal/ke	EVALUATE (Synthesis) institutional/ke	CREATE (Evaluation) Inter-individual/ke
FACTUAL Knowledge	Natural thinking (PoP) Sensorimotor (P) Pre-operational (P) Punishment & Reward Orientation (Ko)					
FACTUAL AND CONCEPTUAL Knowledge		Meaning-making (PoP) Pre-operational and concrete operational (P) punishment and reward orientation and instrumental orientation (Ko)				
CONCEPTUAL AND PROCEDURAL Knowledge			Definition of thinking AND Definition of learning (PoP) Concrete operational & Early formal operational (P) Instrumental Orientation & Interpersonal Concordance Orientation (Ko)	Definition of thinking AND Definition of learning (PoP) Early formal operational (P) Instrumental Orientation & Interpersonal Concordance Orientation (Ko)		
PROCEDURAL AND METACOGNITIVE Knowledge					Responsive cognition (PoP) Full formal operational (P) Societal Orientation (Ko)	
METACOGNITIVE Knowledge						Cognitive agency Successful intelligence AND Wisdom (PoP) Full formal operational & Post-formal/Dialectical (P) Principled Orientation (Ko)

Figure 3.2. Points of Practice: Bloom's and Bloom's Revised Taxonomies; Kegan, Piaget, and Kohlberg Stages Adapted from Kegan (1980); Krathwohl (2002). (Key: b = Bloom; K = Krathwohl; ke = Kegan; Ko = Kohlberg; P = Piaget; PoP = Point of Practice).

turing their thinking and meaning-making throughout the teaching and learning journey to *how to think*.

Traditional public educational practice grows meaning-making and thinking beyond natural limitations. Based on Kegan's (1980) insight that individuals are the context of their own meaning-making, and his depiction of alignment among and across various developmental stages (e.g., meaning-making, cognitive development, moral development), a GPPS takes advantage of research suggesting that student learning is enhanced when educators respond to the maturation of these developmental capacities (Ignelzi, 2000, p. 6).

To make the most of the complex nature of human development via professional practice, educators can once again borrow from the work of Fox and Alexander (2011) to understand that *how to think* is the complex interplay among cognitive behaviors between various layers of cognition within the human brain. Making sense of the world and natural thinking are initial points of practice that allow both students and educators to orient themselves to formative capacities essential to the journey toward *how to think*.

Meanwhile, Back in Class (II)

Returning once again to Mr. Houston's class, meaning-making came into play during the lesson. This class happened to be the Honors Band, comprised predominantly of juniors and seniors in high school.

Mr. Houston brought the emotion and conceptual framework of the piece of music—a moving tribute to the victims, survivors, and heroes of 9/11—into his explanation of the emotional tone to be conveyed when the piece is played. He relied on his assessment of the students' developmental capacities for a combination of early *formal operational thinking operations* and *interpersonal/institutional* development for the complex telling of his own 9/11 experience as a platform from which the students could evoke an effective musical tone and emotion.

Adopting a Definition of Thinking: Point of Practice

Adopting a definition of thinking orients an identification, selection, and application of habits of mind during professional practice. The definition of thinking that was adopted to guide education as a point of practice is provided by Holyoak and Morrison (2005): "Thinking is the systematic transformation of mental representations of knowledge to characterize actual or possible states of the world, often in service of goals" (p. 2).

This definition is certainly not the only definition of thinking that a teacher could adopt but it conveys the effect of professional practice by conjoining cognitive process (systematic transformation) with knowledge (mental representations of knowledge) across the stages of human development. Often, paraphrasing adopted definitions provides educators with a readily available mnemonic device.

The paraphrase for the adopted definition of thinking shared earlier looks like this: *I am teaching students to develop, access, and apply knowledge and cognitive behaviors as successful intelligence for reflection, decisions, creativity, actions, and behavior that balances individual and public goods.*

This adopted definition also conveys the outcome of *how to think* (characterize actual or possible states of the world) in a way that carries points of practice forward, ultimately, to cognitive agency. Traditional public educators already attend to *systematic transformation of mental representations* within quality instruction and engage students with the cognitive behaviors that many refer to as habits of mind (Dewey, 1916; Mezirow, 1997).

Bringing habits of mind into quality instruction occurs when educators manifest the art and science of selected resources and routes crafted together via an adopted definition of thinking. Consider, for a moment, *connecting ideas and/or finding patterns among ideas,* one of the habits of mind listed by Schmoker (2006). Recall of the intersection between knowledge and cognitive process is one way to begin crafting a lesson that focuses on this habit of mind.

The cognitive process of this habit of mind—*connecting ideas* or *finding patterns among ideas*—becomes the "how," the cognitive behavior, of connecting and finding patterns designed or incorporated by a teacher within the lesson. "How" must be accompanied by ideas, the knowledge—*mental representations of knowledge*—among which students make connections or find patterns.

Depending on the grade level, subject area, and learning responses of students, colleagues can teach, talk about, and increase student responsibility for graphic organizers—webs, various note-taking systems, split-screen and compare/contrast graphs—as visual representations that collect and separate knowledge as a platform from which to seek patterns and trends.

Then, the cognitive process and related habits of mind for connecting ideas and identifying patterns can be taught as students identify patterns, connections, similarities, and differences among and between the representations of knowledge provided or accessed during the lesson and placed in the graphic organizer(s). It's important to realize that quality instruction aligned with an adopted definition of thinking should pay attention to what Winstead (2004) terms "automatizing or knowing automatically" (p. 36) habits of mind.

As so many colleagues know, graphic organizers, mnemonics, authentic learning, Venn diagrams, and many other resources and processes facilitate automatic access for students to cognitive behaviors that constitute a knowledge and cognitive dimension continuum from accessing prior knowledge to the acquisition of new knowledge. This automaticization of cognitive behaviors means that what can be described as a retrograde motion of teaching and learning emerges in quality instruction where accessing prior knowledge and cognitive processes allows entry into and acquisition of new knowledge and/or cognitive processes.

Studies reveal the importance to educators of this combination (aligning professional practice with a definition of thinking) and the importance to students of experiencing this instruction (coupled with what's known as effortful learning) (Brown, Roediger, & McDaniel, 2014). The cognitive interplay that's created by instruction that aligns and combines in this way engages the brain to form new synapses between axons and dendrites (Brown, Roediger, & McDaniel, 2014).

Adopting a Definition of Learning: Point of Practice

The good news is that students arrive in classrooms with a treasure trove of individual assets and cognitive wherewithal to make sense of reality and think about information. These capabilities and assets are valuable but relatively inert because *how to think* "requires a level of precision and articulation that must be learned" (Ritchart & Perkins, 2005, p. 776).

The instructional pursuit of a primary purpose imbues a level of precision and articulation within student cognition that "extends beyond a natural processing of the world and into the realm of deliberative thinking acts" (Ritchart & Perkins, 2005, p. 776). Directed and intentional learning, then, is required to take each person's natural cognition and personal assets into higher-order, intentional, deliberative, cognitive interplay.

To help establish deliberative thinking acts in the cognition of students, the next point of practice is a definition of learning. Initially, a weighty definition indicates that learning "is defined holistically as the basic process of human adaptation" (Kolb & Kolb, 2009, p. 42). To link this definition to one suitable for everyday professional practice, Brown et al. (2014) define learning as "acquiring knowledge and skills and having them readily available from memory so you can make sense of future problems and opportunities" (p. 2). Both definitions convey learning as process, which eventuates in making sense of, or adapting to, the varied environments encountered in the world.

The more down to earth of these two definitions (Brown, Roediger, & McDaniel, 2014) conveys, further, that learning is both an acquiring (which necessitates instruction) and an availability (which facilitates agency) for purposeful reflection or action. Mezirow (2000) adds to these important perspectives about learning and provides a cue, in the form of *mindful learning*, about the value of transformational learning on the journey to *how to think*. "Mindful learning is defined by Langer (1997, p. 4) as the continuous creation of new categories, openness to new information, and an implicit awareness of more than one perspective" (p. 7).

This insight allows educators to frame a first question to evaluate their engagement in quality instruction: Does professional practice call forward thinking behaviors that are readily accessible from students' memories?

This definition leads to a second question that evaluates student thinking during professional practice: Are students growing the interplay of their cognitive behaviors to demonstrate making sense of the world with new knowledge and skills that can seek balance between individual and societal goods? These questions, and how traditional public educators respond to them, open the door to a discussion about mindful learning fostered during the last two points of practice, responsive cognition and cognitive agency.

Responsive Cognition: Point of Practice

Traditional public educators take responsibility for engaging students with cognitive behaviors whose interplay establishes the conditions necessary to create new knowledge as an essential characteristic of *how to think*. Meaning-making and natural thinking are the wellspring of natural cognitive behaviors.

Natural thinking and meaning-making carry limitations that only the process of human adaptation can affect if *how to think* is to occur. Taking students to cognitive behaviors acquired through the influence of professional practice in traditional public education classrooms requires that model-of and model-for instruction are guided by definitions of thinking and learning. With this interaction among the first four points of practice under way, cognitive behaviors develop as *responsive cognition*.

Responsive cognition is student mental work, the cognitive behaviors accessed and expressed during teaching based on definitions of thinking and learning in a confluence of knowledge, cognitive process, natural thinking, meaning-making, and habits of mind. Larson and Angus (2011) identify this mental work as "cognitive tools, including insights, precepts, knowledge, and action schemas" (p. 277).

Meanwhile, Back in Class (III)

Guided by definitions of thinking and learning, Mr. Houston's instruction required mental work from students in band class that called upon critical examination of evidence in a text/score; dealing with complex information; speculating; explaining; and/or finding patterns among ideas.

It is the responsibility of traditional public education to create classroom learning experiences and activities as thinking-scapes in which student mental work grows to express the depth and breadth of thinking required in a democracy to balance individual and public goods. Under these conditions of quality instruction, multiple habits of mind interplay as responsive cognition. In this way, how to think constructs a bridge, cognitive agency, from the individual good of matured cognitive capacities balanced by seeking the public good.

Cognitive Agency: Point of Practice

Quality instruction has the power to engage students in the process of human adaptation and establish responsive cognition whereby *how to think* becomes integral to an individual's meaning-making. Responsive cognition engenders our sixth point of practice, *cognitive agency*.

Cognitive agency describes the synergy of responsive cognition with overt behaviors chosen to balance individual and public goods. Cognitive agency rounds out the points of practice because it is congruent with a sociocultural imperative of U.S. democracy that is most simply illustrated by our nation's motto, *e pluribus unum*.

From many diverse, socially responsible thinkers come cognitive behaviors capable of evolving the greater good, in the form of a more perfect union, when traditional public education fosters *how to think* for all students. The motto of the United States symbolizes the overriding value of cognitive agency, responsive cognition, natural thinking, individual assets, and meaning-making when these characteristics are influenced by quality instruction anchored by definitions of thinking and learning in traditional public education.

QUALITY INSTRUCTION

Remember THAT colleague who was all about theory? A time comes when the application of theory, putting concepts into practice, takes center stage in function for traditional public education. It's time to take the insights of THAT colleague and think practically. How does quality instruction bring the concepts and theories and ideas discussed so far into day-to-day practice on behalf of each student?

Traditional public education colleagues accept responsibility for improving and growing each student's capacity for thinking and meaning-making. Based on definitions of thinking and learning, educators can make decisions about instruction to equip students with the capacity to access and express complex cognitive interplay across points of practice and throughout the stages of human development.

For instance, an adopted definition of thinking helps design lessons that develop interplay among habits of mind. Quality instruction depends upon the alignment between the primary purpose of traditional public education and cognitive capacity with the adopted definition of thinking.

Teaching Style Matters More Than Learning Style

Quality instruction doesn't need to align with what are usually called *learning styles*, the perceived learning strengths of students. On the contrary, because "people do have multiple forms of intelligence to bring to bear on learning, and you learn best when you 'go wide,' drawing on all of your aptitudes and resourcefulness" (Brown, Roediger, & McDaniel, 2014, p. 4), quality instruction depends on knowing that learning is an ongoing process of revisiting old learning, updating what's been learned before, and connecting the old and the updated with new knowledge (Brown, Roediger, & McDaniel, 2014). Interconnections between points of practice and habits of mind reviewed, taught, applied, and extended within lessons provide a conceptual framework for the practical in decisions and responses that constitute teaching styles.

The process of human adaptation via classroom experiences that connect what's been learned already with updated knowledge (often expressed via different habits of mind that constitute new knowledge) is captured in day-to-day examples including: teaching kindergarten students to predict what comes next in a story; engaging high school students with qualitative analysis in chemistry; dialoguing with students in another country over the Internet about the day-to-day life of a fifth grader; or alluding to a theme from classic literature in writing to persuade a local official to improve a policy.

Public educators understand that human development and *how to think* evolve; both are influenced in transformative ways when led out by traditional public education.

Traditional public education elevates the process of human adaptation to the point that "thinking is directed toward achieving some desired state of affairs, some goal that motivates the thinker to perform mental work" (Holyoak & Morrison, 2005, p. 2).

During Quality Instruction

Quality instruction in traditional public education puts students in classroom situations designed to apply habits of mind toward some desired state of affairs. The motivation of instruction augmented by wonder, questions, unknowns, problems, and or authentic dilemmas invites mental work that "'occurs as students actively assimilate new information and experiences and construct their own meanings (National Council of Teachers of Mathematics, 1991, p. 2)'" (USDOE, 2000, p. 26).

Quality instruction inspires mental work and the construction of "their own meanings" for each student as cognitive interplay of habits of mind establish responsive cognition. Quality instruction engages students with explanations and explorations of, and through, habits of mind.

This mental work allows the brain to set the stage with *recall and remember*. Quality instruction that is based on definitions of thinking and learning functions as a generator that powers the interplay of cognitive behaviors, the student mental work, to construct new knowledge and new meanings.

To realize these outcomes, quality instruction must promote the maturation of existing habits of mind to explore and teach new knowledge and cognitive process. Lessons that engage students among and between cognitive process and knowledge dimensions co-exist with stages of human development. These lessons invite students into tasks that call for cognitive interplay that resolves dissonance, calls forth creativity, fosters social justice, makes judgments, evaluates circumstances, solves problems, collaborates, and/or sustains valid and ethical propositions.

These classroom experiences also can ask "big" questions, pose conundrums, establish personal connections, activate mysteries, engage in simulations, and/or examine authentic problems. Decisions and behaviors of public education colleagues about quality instruction create *thinking-scapes* in the classroom. These teaching and learning vistas always include the individual cognitive and experiential assets of each student.

It is this precision and articulation in quality instruction that facilitates individual capacity to "construct a developmental 'bridge' between the student's current way of understanding and the new way, thus providing a path on which to cross over (Kegan, 1994)" (Ignelzi, 2000, p. 6).

Quality instruction puts students in a position, cognitively speaking, to call forth what they remember, engage remembered habits of mind that apply to instructional asks and tasks, accommodate additional instruction about previously unlearned habits of mind, and apply new habits of mind and/or new knowledge to think into any of a variety of applied or authentic outcomes. Traditional public education colleagues create cognitive bridge-building capacity for the meaning-making of each student.

Learning Beyond: Transformative Learning Theory

How to think forestalls the limitations that typify the cognitive box canyon of natural thinking. Among the resources available to public educators, several theories serve to empower instruction that leads student learning out of cognitive dead ends. Transformative learning theory is one of these because it incorporates core elements such as "individual experience, critical reflection, dialogue, holistic orientation, context, and authentic relationships (Taylor, 2009)" (English & Irving, 2012, p. 250).

These elements tend to give thinkers the ability to "move toward a frame of reference that is more inclusive, discriminating, self-reflective, and integrative of experience" (Mezirow, 1997, p. 5). Thinking about teaching and learning, about responsive cognition and cognitive agency, about human development, and about the public good puts this theory into both model-of and model-for perspectives about instruction throughout this book.

WHAT TRADITIONAL PUBLIC EDUCATORS CAN DO: INVEST IN QUALITY PROFESSIONAL PRACTICE!

Although it is beyond the scope of this primer to discuss all the important factors that compose quality instruction, this discussion of intelligence, habits of mind, and points of practice provides a starting point for crafting professional practices that gather information and apply cognitive processes to engage learners with *how to think*. This primer reflects the notion that learners—both educators and students—can gather and employ the full range of personal assets and the complexity of function designed and expressed in the classroom.

Instruction, it must be asserted, is not a regimented or lock-step process; teaching and learning on the journey toward *how to think* depends on professional practices crafted through *function*. Function will be discussed later and contrasted with the antithesis of teaching and learning riveted to free market theory that drives privatization/choice education.

Professional practice in traditional public education relies on theories, data, selected definitions, and research-based strategies. Making the most of these factors, points of practice are a GPPS to guide the transformative nature of professional practice that establishes the interplay of cognitive behaviors for students. And, traditional public education colleagues may use or design points of practice as next steps into new knowledge for professional practice as suggested in these examples:

1. *How to think* depends on learning to access and remember information while acquiring the ability to mesh other cognitive behaviors with the retrieval of the memory that "holds" this prior learning. In any subject area, at any grade level, knowledge development and training the memory to be able to access information—beginning from each student's baseline of natural thinking and meaning-making—need to be ongoing instructional activities.
2. Selected habits of mind constitute the scaffolding for both model-of and model-for lessons that engage and grow natural thinking and meaning-making. Information-use and memory training are examples of the habits of mind that, when taught and applied in class, give students cognitive "fuel" to drive cognitive interplay on the pathway to *how to think*. While it is beyond the scope of our narra-

tive to explore the full measure of instructional applications available about information-use and memory training, colleagues will gain important insights from the work of Brown et al. (2014).
3. *Lessons that convey priority information* and apply instructional tactics that build memory and the independent learning skills of students shared in the work of Fisher and Frey (2008) can be implemented by asking students to (a) *Begin by answering an "info question" such as* (i) What are the five most important reasons for the start of World War I from the point of view of people in Europe at that time? (ii) What do critics say are the three most powerful writing techniques Hemingway used? (iii) Why is the periodic table of elements organized into general categories, usually depicted by color-coding in the table? (iv) What safety steps are most important to take BEFORE using a miter saw? (b) *Design instruction for practice and interleaving:* (i) Create a pattern- or mnemonic-creating opportunity that helps students remember the five causes of World War I they identified from the point of view of European citizens. (ii) Develop a way for students to understand and remember the three writing techniques identified in class. (iii) Design a way for others to remember accurately the general categories in the periodic table. (iv) Establish a "memory anchor" that anyone can use to review the miter saw safety steps before they use the saw. (c) *Create a way to evaluate and re-teach and/or enrich the information you identified.* (b) *Take the lesson to a next level by engaging students in the application of information and memory to deal with a more complex question derived from an "info question" such as those shared above in i, ii, iii, and iv* (Fisher & Frey, 2008).
4. *In addition to* the elements of a GPPS that orient decisions about instructional behaviors, it can be helpful to use landmarks to further ensure that instruction is on track. Madeline Hunter's lesson design landmarks remain some of the most effective of these additions to any GPPS.
5. The elements of Hunter's design—*anticipatory set; objective and purpose; input; modeling; checking for understanding; guided practice; and independent practice* (Hunter, 1982; Marzano, 2007, p. 181)—establish ways to monitor and adjust the pace of instruction, provide a format in which to apply relevant habits of mind, engage ongoing evaluation of student thinking, and connect with other, different, writers and scholars who also have thought about effective landmarks (Fisher & Frey, 2008).

TEACHER SNAPSHOT: SENOR BEROVIDES

Early in my career, teaching at an urban elementary school, I learned from my colleague Eduardo Berovides how vital it is to know, understand, and value students for the cognitive and experiential assets they bring to school every day. Senor Berovides was born in Cuba and came to the United States with his family while still a youngster. He talked about his reactions when school adults treated him as a person endowed with a rich variety of thinking skills united with and expressed in his cultural, family, and personal background. Senor Berovides also recounted different, devastating, teacher behaviors based on the assumption that he was less capable than majority students in the class.

Senor Berovides incorporated the lives of our students in math lessons that put the multiple cultures of students from our school's attendance area into the forefront as examples of strength, creativity, intellect, and capability. A veteran educator, Senor Berovides was phenomenally patient with my questions and modeled his incorporation of student assets for his rookie colleague daily since we worked in an open concept school. His professional engagement with all students established a model-for of interaction and instruction that I did my best to emulate from that point forward.

WHAT TRADITIONAL PUBLIC EDUCATORS CAN DO: TALK ABOUT QUALITY INSTRUCTION!

Identifying and using points of practice while organizing habits of mind using Bloom's Taxonomy puts traditional public educators in a position to orient quality instructional practice. This activity constitutes an analysis and an evaluation of where traditional public educators find themselves. At the same time, a GPPS gives parents and caregivers an opportunity to understand the value of the pursuit of *how to think* on behalf of their child(ren). Putting a GPPS to work is accomplished in several ways:

- *Include the paraphrase* of key definitions—or some similar "cue" about what goes on in class to engage students with *how to think*—in communications with parents and caregivers. Paraphrases carry the quality practice of education while avoiding "shop talk" or "education-ese."
- *Explaining a primary purpose* should be among the first things done each school year. And this explanation should be shared and shared again over the course of every school year.
- *Back-to-school night* or parent/teacher conferences give an example to parents and caregivers of their child's success with some aspect of thinking behaviors or the interplay of these behaviors. Throughout the school year include illustrations of how and when these behaviors benefit students now and in the future.

- *When a student needs* remedial support in a subject area or with some aspect of thinking behaviors, share with parents/caregivers how new or second-chance instruction addresses the area(s) for improvement.
- *Sharing how work in the classroom* segues with a child's response-to-instruction is not only a way to tell parents/caregivers how well a teacher knows their child but it's also another way to avoid "shop talk." Talk about "my response to your child's learning."
- *During work* with colleagues at grade level and/or in a subject area, an agreed-upon definition of thinking allows collaboration about how best to incorporate thinking behaviors into function and grade-level, department, or team progression-of-instruction.
- *Interconnecting and reinforcing* instruction across subject areas or classrooms to engage students in habits of mind—using information about each student's previous and ongoing progress—means maximizing the learning of all students.
- *Buy THAT Colleague* an Extra Soda! Quality instruction depends on the intersection of a dynamic set of ideas, constructs, and theories. Devote time to explanations from THAT colleague to enrich and guide the practical implementation of lessons.

Putting Knowledge and Cognitive Process to Work

Traditional public education colleagues must make meaningful choices among resources and routes on the way to *how to think*. The choices of greatest significance to students lie in educators' successful intelligence employed during instruction across points of practice. Function of the professional practice in traditional public education is oriented by meaning-making, natural thinking, definitions of thinking and learning, responsive cognition, and cognitive agency.

The difficult work that is quality instruction and professional practice, teaching occurs when colleagues think and act to establish function. The primary purpose of traditional public education emerging via function engages all students in multiple cognitive capacities required to navigate successfully the infinite choices of adulthood in a democracy.

Professional excellence depends on informed choices that represent colleagues' successful intelligence. Choice, in traditional public education, is neither mechanical nor ideological. Instead, traditional public educators make choices devoted to function that put *how to think* at the forefront of cognitive behaviors of enduring value to students and to U.S. democracy.

FOUR
The Mechanisms Sold as Education in the Free Market

The last thing American students deserve is a saw applied to the tree where traditional public education is perched out on a limb. Almost 90 percent of all students in the United States attend traditional public school. Traditional public education has the capacity necessary for model-of and model-for quality that serves all students throughout the current century. But, traditional public educators must know about the free market for education and its advocates to understand how the profession got out on a limb in the first place.

Traditional public educators are confronted by free market theory, and the proponents of this perspective, who advocate for choice education or privatization. Free market theory adherents approach the limb where traditional public education finds itself with a saw and malice aforethought. This is neither new news nor fake news.

Traditional public education is in a tenuous position daily despite a near monopoly on public schools in America that even free market proponents acknowledge. This may seem surprising or even unlikely, but the mere presence of free market theory and its continuing impact makes it tremendously important to ask: How did traditional public education, democracy's fuel, end up teetering on the edge?

In no small measure, traditional public education is out on a limb because too little is known about, and too little attention is paid to, the purpose and goals of free market theory. Moreover, too little emphasis is given to the funding and finance devoted to replacing traditional public education with choice schooling. To close this information gap, this chapter examines the free market, its proponents, and its impact.

FREE MARKET THEORY AND THINKING

Free market theory is a belief system "that schools (public sector) should be run like businesses (private sector), [which] while lacking any evidentiary warrant, has become a new 'common sense' among a wide swath of the American public (Cuban, 2004; Goodsell, 2004; Mautner, 2010)" (Anderson & Donchik, 2016, p. 337). A free market for education hypothesized by privatization adherents embraces less government and forswears regulation in the conviction that less government means lower taxes and fewer regulations promise greater individual freedom.

Beneficent claims like this about the free market camouflage a view of America and its education as rooted in survival of the fittest, funded by massive amounts of cash. Free market theory embraces the denial of "'the importance of public goods or else maintains that all our goods are best achieved by individuals acting out of individual self-interest'" (Hostetler, 2003, p. 355).

A dilemma arises for traditional public education from this focal point. Education in the free market is "concerned less with measuring whether schools help students learn and more with whether parents have an opportunity to pick a school for their children" (Brown, 2017). This belief sidetracks a purpose for and quality of traditional public education because free market theory directs advantages toward adults instead of students.

The allure of self-aggrandizement makes market theory attractive to those with the capacity to take advantage. Without paying attention to this misdirection and without pursuing a primary purpose via quality instruction, traditional public educators virtually invite those carrying the saw to climb toward the limb.

Mechanisms: Education in the Free Market

Free market theory advocates the demise of public education—labeled as "government schools"—and the ascension of teaching and learning synonymous with various mechanisms including *vouchers, charter schools, tax credits,* and *education savings plans.*

- "Think of traditional vouchers as coupons, backed by state dollars, that parents can use to send their kids to the school of their choice, even private, religiously affiliated schools" (Barnum, 2017a). Some critics have referred to this mechanism as a "backpack full of cash" that every new choice school covets because each child brings it with them when they transfer schools (Walsh, 2017).
- Charter schools are "publicly funded, privately operated schools that families can select outside of their zoned schools. They promise

greater school-level autonomy in exchange for greater accountability" (Loeb, Valant, & Kasman, 2011, p. 143).
- "Tax credit programs usually offer individuals or corporations tax credits if they donate to a scholarship granting organization which in turn offers private school scholarships based on various criteria, including income" (Klein, 2017, pp. 2–3).
- Education savings plans are often understood as meeting only the description given to one type of plan—the 529 plan—by the U.S. Securities and Exchange Commission, which indicates that "a 529 plan is a tax-advantaged savings plan designed to encourage saving for future college costs" (U.S. Securities and Exchange Commission, nd). Coverdell Education Savings Accounts perform the same function but permit dollars to be set aside for private K–12 education.

Seventeen U.S. states offer tax credit programs, and fourteen states along with the District of Columbia offer voucher programs (Klein, 2017). Forty-four states and the District of Columbia have laws that permit charter schools (Education Commission of the States, 2018).

The Free Market, Its Mechanisms, and Foolishness

The value in knowing *how to think* and developing successful intelligence lies in boosting the cognitive capacity of all students beyond the lower-order cognitive behaviors that predominate in uneducated natural thinking and meaning-making. The primary purpose of traditional public education is important because, as Sternberg, Reznitskaya, and Jarvin (2007) confirm, "one can be smart but foolish" (p. 144).

Foolishness, as these authors describe it, is found in the thinking and behaviors represented by six fallacies: unrealistic optimism, egocentrism, omniscience, omnipotence, invulnerability, and ethical disengagement (Sternberg, Reznitskaya, & Jarvin 2007, pp. 144–145). This discussion about the free market will examine the relationship between mechanisms and these fallacies.

For now, it's important to realize that omniscience is the first of the fallacies of foolishness riveted to free market theory. Free market schooling proponents categorically deny the value of traditional public education and use the free market agenda—e.g., less government, lower taxes, limited regulation, choice—to rally policy-makers. Policy-making dedicated to free market schooling puts traditional public education in a vulnerable position.

Traditional public education becomes vulnerable if only because no claim of omniscience, or omnipotence, arises from our purpose and quality in that function is anchored by continuous improvement. Traditional public education is consistently vulnerable under the political circumstances engendered by free market theory because natural thinking, my-side bias, and/or foolishness perpetuate themselves.

FIVE

Let's Meet Two Advocates for Free Market Schooling

Too few traditional public educators realize that free market theory is a well-funded and ballyhooed perspective about schooling for America's students. This chapter introduces two advocates for free market schooling. These proponents symbolize the influence and power brought to bear when free market theory is offered as what's best for teaching and learning in the United States. The first free market advocate is known as ALEC.

INTRODUCING ALEC

ALEC is the American Legislative Exchange Council. Active since the 1970s, ALEC seeks to establish less government in all aspects of society, including education.

ALEC "is a partnership internally—or perhaps more correctly, a strategic alliance—and externally a node within a larger network of think tanks, corporate lobbyists, venture philanthropists, and advocacy organizations that together form part of this new modality of governance" (Anderson & Donchik, 2016, p. 327). Members of ALEC are representatives of large U.S. corporations and state legislators who collaborate to design and share model legislation for adoption at the state level across the United States (Anderson & Donchik, 2016).

ALEC "seeks to undermine public education by systematically defunding and ultimately destroying public education as we know it" (Underwood & Mead, 2012, p. 1). The impact of this approach is exemplified by Indiana's ALEC-influenced approach to traditional public education where "in the rush to overhaul education, state lawmakers abandoned decades of commitment to the traditional public school system, pushing forward even as districts started closing schools, cutting programs, and losing teachers" (Herron & Fittes, 2017, p. 6A).

The free market for U.S. education envisioned by ALEC is an environment overflowing with consumer choice and competition among schools (Binelli, 2017). ALEC and its allies aspire to impose a free market for U.S. schooling where risk-taking and an entrepreneurial panache predominate.

For ALEC and its allies the private sector promotes choices in a free market of schooling that spawn competition among schools for student enrollment, which in turn yields efficiency. Efficiency, ideological proof that less is more, is an article of faith without which the reform of the public sector—traditional public education—is not complete.

ALEC's promise of reform and freedom in U.S. schooling comes to the fore via free market agenda items including reducing education cost/taxes, deconstructing teacher unions, establishing profit-making opportunities for free market advocates, and installing mechanisms to enable school choice (Underwood & Mead, 2012). To push this agenda forward, ALEC employs impressions about freedom, rights, and choice to disguise the organization's intent to "shift from the democratic notion of universal citizenship rights/identities to a system of individual consumer rights/identities" (Anderson & Donchik, 2016, p. 341).

One Big Happy Free Market Family

ALEC is a part of a larger network of organizations, foundations, and individuals dedicated to creating a free market for U.S. education (Hefling, 2017; Mayer, 2017). A significant part of this family includes one-fourth of all state legislators who are members of ALEC.

This helps explain why so many state statutes reflect the priorities in ALEC's agenda. Model bills are prepared by ALEC members and passed along to state legislatures for ratification to "influence teacher certification, teacher evaluation, collective bargaining, curriculum, funding, special education, student assessment" (Underwood & Mead, 2012, p. 3).

The influence of ALEC and others in this ideological family is expressed in state regulations and statutes that allow transferring state tax payments away from public education to private or for-profit educational entities, ending the influence of unions in public education, curtailing certification requirements, and imposing private sector management expectations on public schools (Anderson & Donchik, 2016).

INTRODUCING BETSY DEVOS

Betsy DeVos represents the individuals and families across the United States with staggering wealth who nurture free market schooling and the legislation that supports this perspective. A venture philanthropist long before she became U.S. Secretary of Education, DeVos is the poster child for families like hers who have long dedicated time and funding to advocate for "extreme free-market economic theories rejecting government intervention" (Mayer, 2017, p. 283).

A hint about the extent to which her family's considerable fortune is employed in support of a free market is captured in her co-founding an advocacy group for school choice, the American Federation for Children (Hefling, 2017). DeVos once shared the belief that the time had arrived to retire Detroit's traditional public schools and liberate the students in the city to take advantage of school choice (Zernike, 2016).

DeVos's decades of influence on education in Michigan led the *Detroit Free Press* to editorialize that her lobbying effort on behalf of free market schooling for Detroit engendered a "deeply dysfunctional education landscape—where failure is rewarded with opportunities for expansion and 'choice' means the opposite for tens of thousands of children" (Mead, 2016).

The intensity of this devotion to the free market earned DeVos unvarnished descriptions from those who researched her perspective on schooling. "She is, in essence, a lobbyist—someone who has used her extraordinary wealth to influence the conversation about education reform, and to bend that conversation to her ideological convictions despite the dearth of evidence supporting them" (Strauss, 2015).

Funding for Free Market Schooling

During the summer of 2016, DeVos and her family accessed their personal fortune and "contributed $1.45 million over two months—an astonishing average of $25,000 a day—to Michigan GOP lawmakers and the state party after the Republican-led Legislature derailed a bipartisan provision that would have provided more charter school oversight in Detroit" (Strauss, 2015).

Like the rest of her networked free market brethren, DeVos has cash at the ready to force-feed privatization of U.S. schooling "on the ground at the state level where the network can disrupt the educational status quo" (Hefling, 2017, p. 2). DeVos understands the authority of state legislatures over education. She and her husband donated tens of thousands of dollars to the political campaigns of governors in Arizona, Tennessee, Indiana, New Mexico, North Carolina, Illinois, Florida, and Michigan (Ujifusa, 2016).

The use of significant cash resources to influence public opinion, legislators' inclinations, and political processes are not strategies unique to the DeVos family. Americans for Prosperity and the Libre Initiative are two examples of the massive fiscal resources of the Koch brothers that are brought to bear on behalf of the free market. For instance, in Arizona funding from the Libre Initiative quashed a referendum designed to benefit traditional public education; the referendum sought to prevent the diversion of millions of state dollars away from traditional public schools to choice education.

In Colorado, the Libre Initiative's financial support promoted charter schools and education savings accounts. Finally, resources from these deep pockets funded media in Virginia that criticized the gubernatorial candidate of the Democratic Party (the ultimate victor) because he opposed education savings accounts (Hefling, 2017, p. 3).

WHAT'S FOR SALE IN THE FREE MARKET OF SCHOOLING?

The cascade of dollars to support the free market of schooling flows in a multitude of directions, including "charter schools, online schools, virtual schools, blended learning, any combination thereof—and, frankly, any combination, or any kind of choice that hasn't yet been thought of" (Mead, 2016).

Prodigious investments by well-heeled individuals and families to create what appears to be a free-for-all for schooling are not random or spontaneous investments. Advocacy for privatization of education via the free market in the United States constitutes nothing less than a shift in "power towards private policy elites" and away from traditional public origins for, and intentions of, educational policy in our democracy (Lubienski, 2013). For individuals like DeVos and for organizations like ALEC, this objective constitutes a long-sought-after ROI (return on investment).

Significant networking is under way among free market proponents as represented by like-minded foundations, plutocrats like the Koch brothers, various networks (ALEC, for instance), family- and ideologically based foundations, and the Council for National Policy, "a little-known club of a few hundred of the most powerful conservatives in the country" (Mayer, 2017, p. 286).

Those who participate in the effort to establish free market schooling throughout the United States contribute many millions to support policies, mechanisms, and ROI designed to "take public dollars . . . away from the existing public schools, effectively creating a two-tier educational system that could hurt the students most in need" (Rich, 2014). Dollars from free market advocates are expended not only on constructing mechanisms but also on advertising, marketing programs, curricular and instructional materials, as well as lobbying for choice education (Elder, 2014).

Free Market Shop Talk

Impressions and coded language—the shop talk of free market theory proponents—entice policy-makers, politicians, and parents/caregivers to be a part of what is referred to in this book as *stealth-schooling* for U.S. students. ALEC and its members who draft the model bills understand that the strategic use of language can help to create or reinforce a new common sense as well as make their passage more likely. Edelman (1978) called this "the linguistic structuring of social problems" (Anderson & Donchik, 2016, p. 343). Language is the key to tracking ALEC's footprint in the forest of any state's legislation.

Because ALEC's membership is secret, the language of state statutes provides clues that reveal the extent to which ALEC, and not the electorate, linguistically structures a state's laws about education. Specific vocabulary contained in the titles and verbiage of state statutes about education (e.g., *choice, freedom, rights, accountability, innovation, family, scholarships*) signals ALEC's influence (Anderson & Donchik, 2016).

The titles of model bills cooked up by ALEC are laden with coded language, implying benefits for all but delivering rewards for a select few. Some of these titles and their subliminal agenda messages (shown in *italics*) include: National Teacher Certification *Fairness* Act, Teacher *Choice* Compensation Act, Parental *Choice* Scholarship Program Act, *Smart* Start *Scholarship* Program, *Parental Rights* Act, *Great* Schools Tax Credit, and *Virtual Public Schools* Act (Underwood & Mead, 2012).

Talking the Talk, Walking the Free Market Walk

The subterfuge encapsulated in structuring of social problems—and traditional public education is certainly a problem from the point of view of free market proponents—is illustrated in the *Education Accountability Act*, a model bill drafted by ALEC.

Without understanding the free market agenda, and without knowing that those who would destroy traditional public education utilize linguistic structuring, the title of this model bill implies the creation of a statutory basis for keeping schools accountable. At first glance the title seems benign except for a bit of legislative overkill since multiple accountability processes apply throughout traditional public education.

But, taking time to apply knowledge about ALEC and the ideological impressions inserted in model bills reveals how traditional public education constitutes a mammoth "social problem" that demands to be "structured" from the perspective of ALEC and other ideologues.

This bill establishes "consequences of not meeting the designated standards. These consequences include declaring a school 'educationally bankrupt,' replacing the faculty, or issuing the parents of its students a voucher to subsidize attendance at a non-public school" (Anderson & Donchik, 2016, p. 346). Because free market–aligned legislation is festooned with coded language, traditional public educators need to know the language because the intended destruction of traditional public education captured in statute and rule at the state level by this language is rendered all but invisible to the uninformed eye.

SIX

The Sinkhole That Is Context of the Free Market

Mechanisms and context are one and the same in the free market of schooling. Vouchers, charter schools, and tax credits are context for education. Free market theory and the proponents of free market schooling do not differentiate the two.

As a result, free market schooling operates above an expanding sinkhole. The context of free market schooling establishes a vast emptiness because mechanisms are disconnected from and have no impact on the practices, qualities, and purpose necessary for all students to attain successful intelligence. Infatuated with context, proponents fail to perceive that the mechanisms of free market schooling are auto-eroding.

Proponents of the free market look past data and research; ignore the relationship between *how to think* and democracy; and bypass student futures in lieu of profit and policy. Implementation of the free market pays no heed to the teaching and learning lacuna beneath its mechanisms because overinvestment in context is paramount in choice schooling.

Privatization advocates purposely buy in to the severe limitations of context. Enamored of the ideological trappings, settings, fiscal benefits, and structures of the free market, adherents promote mechanisms as the necessary and sufficient be-all and end-all of choice schooling.

The purpose of this chapter is to contend against context. Traditional public educators reject context as a primary purpose. Context alone is inertia—and education, *leading out,* is and must be a matter of continuous improvement.

Moreover, function, quality professional practice, is part and parcel of the ethos for educating that allows traditional public education to be transformative. The response from the American public when the context-centric myopia of privatization becomes obvious is worth understanding. A sinkhole beneath privatization awaits students and families whose hopes and futures dangle unaware above the empty spaces of free market context.

THE LIMITATIONS OF FREE MARKET CONTEXT

Once free market proponents present context as the operational superiority of choice schooling, mechanisms become the comparative that true believers use to assert that traditional public education is worthless. Without offering a data-based counterargument to this bluff, traditional public educators risk underestimating the power of facts, details, and research that lie within quality and function. As it turns out, the data-free zone in which free market schooling chooses to exist does not appear to bamboozle the general U.S. public.

Data from across the nation indicates how the sinkhole offered by ideologues does not earn the trust of U.S. citizens and families. Several attempts to establish statewide voucher programs were rejected in no uncertain terms.

Voters in Nebraska, Colorado, California, Washington, and Michigan defeated statewide voucher ballot initiatives; when the legislature in Utah passed a law that allowed state funding of school vouchers, voters used a referendum to upend the statute (Burbank & Levin, 2015). When Florida and Oklahoma attempted a repeal of Blaine Amendments ("which prohibit states from spending public money on religious schools and can limit a state's ability to fund private school choice programs" [Wermund, 2016]), voters defeated these ballot initiatives.

By comparison, surveys of public opinion suggest that when parents/caregivers assess the foundation from which local traditional public schools provide teaching and learning, few concerns arise. "While Americans are often pessimistic about the state of American education in the abstract, they tend to be more optimistic about the quality of their local public schools" (Burbank & Levin, 2015, p. 1172).

Those who summarize the survey conducted each year by Phi Delta Kappa share the same finding. As the second decade of the twenty-first century neared an end, more than 60 percent of traditional public school parents and 49 percent of the general public reported that their local traditional public schools deserved a grade of "A" or "B" (PDK, 2017). However, only 24 percent of those responding gave overall traditional public education in the United States an "A" or a "B" (PDK, 2017).

Once traditional public educators realize that parents, caregivers, community members, and others stand beside them in the pursuit of our primary purpose, this information becomes the cues and clues necessary for raising awareness. Data and information about the successes of local public schools constitute what educators require for generalizing and for illustrating the potential for purpose and quality in all traditional public schools.

Overinvestment in Policy for the Free Market

Despite public affinity for the purpose and outcomes of traditional public education, the fiscal clout of free market adherents turns the heads of state legislators across the nation. These policy-makers have a powerful impact on traditional public education.

Policy-makers have the authority to endow traditional public education with the means to deliver the promises of a bright future maximized when each student knows *how to think*, or the authority to strip comprehensive traditional public education of its purpose and to destroy the synergy for balance between individual and public goods.

Despite ample evidence of the negative outcomes of choice schooling and the failure of free market mechanisms to engage the academic growth of all students, policy-makers devote considerable energy to the validation of context via statutes and rules. The result is overinvestment in privatization to the detriment of U.S. students and to the disenfranchisement of voters.

Overinvestment and Policy Bubbles

Jones, Thomas, and Wolfe (2014) identify overinvestment as a situation where the negative outcomes of a policy exceed its costs. Overinvestment means that proponents of a policy arrive at an all-or-nothing-at-all judgment about the value of that policy regardless of cost.

When this happens, cost—which in the case of the free market includes not only financial outlays but also deleterious educational effects and negative societal outcomes—is rendered invisible to those who are all-in for choice schooling.

Mindless obeisance to the context of the free market, with little interest in or reference to its significant negative features, means that policy-makers don't have to reflect or evaluate but can abide with policy-making that "justifies a more-or-less consistent course of sustained policy action" (Jones, Thomas, & Wolfe, 2014, p. 151). Free market context is nothing less than an investment in sustained, self-serving inertia.

As state legislators overinvest in privatization to the point that its promises are fulfilled in negative outcomes and increasing costs, the result is a policy bubble (Jones, Thomas, & Wolfe, 2014). As the name implies, policy bubbles have gossamer-thin value and a tendency to expand nevertheless.

A policy bubble grows without regard to increasing negative outcomes. Mesmerized by the self-aggrandizement promised by the context of and agenda for the free market, policy-makers and privatization proponents do not care about the deleterious effects of the bubble's continued existence.

Overinvestment in free market theory and the policy bubble created across the United States has the unique distinction of creating a positive impact for adherents that is, at the same time, an exorbitant cost for the 90 percent of students not enrolled in choice schooling.

State legislators throughout the United States continue to use ALEC's model bills to impose the free market agenda for schooling. Negative effects on U.S. students of this overinvestment are justified by free market proponents because this small cost is a validation for what amounts to ROI: implementation of free market priorities.

EVALUATING THE POLICY BUBBLE FOR THE FREE MARKET

Four evaluative criteria identified in the research of Jones, Thomas, and Wolfe (2014) allow an assessment of the extent to which overinvestment and a policy bubble are at work on behalf of free market theory. The application of these four criteria (each criterion is shown in italics) evaluates the extent of overinvestment in the privatization policy bubble:

- *"Difficulty in measuring the connection between the instrument and the outcome"* (Jones, Thomas, & Wolfe, 2014, p. 152). It pays to remember that mechanisms, as context, are both means and ends for free market schooling proponents.

  Measuring the link between context of the free market (the instrument) and teaching and learning (viable outcomes worth measuring for any school) are not a priority because measurements are unnecessary. Mechanisms need no measurement to ascertain a connection with an outcome because mechanisms are themselves the outcome of greatest value in free market schooling.

  Mechanisms, as the context of free market theory, connect instrument and outcome automatically. Context in the free market is its own assessment of worth. For all intents and purposes, the automatic value assigned by free market schooling to context bestows value on any characteristic or variable of stealth-schooling.

  Measurement in this case devolves into an article of ideological faith; means/instrument and ends/outcomes are synonymous. Measurement difficulties proliferate, however, if the circular reasoning of ideological validation is jettisoned and attempts are made to calculate a link between mechanisms and student achievement.

  Any attempt to measure a connection between standardized testing (recommended by ALEC as the instrument of greatest value for determining student academic proficiency) and robust student achievement as an outcome is a fool's errand. This task is not just difficult, it is impossible. This impossibility begins with the fact that standardized tests are academically bankrupt; achievement (much less *how to think*) is not measured effectively by standardized testing (Butrymowicz, 2013a).

Nevertheless, free market proponents use the results from standardized tests to confirm the failure of traditional public education. The irony of this comparison lies in data that reveals that students in free market schooling earn either lower or similar results. Again, using Indiana, the Hoosier state, as an example, just as no research establishes a valid or reliable connection between vouchers and positive educational quality, no measure identifies a connection between vouchers and better academic outcomes for Indiana students.

In fact, research found that student achievement was affected negatively by enrollment in choice schooling in the Hoosier state (Singer, 2017). Unfortunately, the inability to measure a connection between significant academic achievement and choice schooling has little impact on overinvestment in free market theory.

- *"People become cognitively and emotionally invested in the means rather than valuing the instrumental value of the means in accomplishing a policy goal"* (Jones, Thomas, & Wolfe, 2014, p. 153). Privatization proponents have little use for the instrumental value of means because they identify means as ends unto themselves.

When this happens, a massive fissure develops between the two factions—on the one side, the emotional commitment to means as the ends of privatization and, on the other side, means as merely an instrument or tool necessary to reach substantial policy goals. The emotional attachment of policy-makers to choice schooling is illustrated when data about negative achievement results, financial mismanagement, or the erosion of inalienable rights fail to deter the fervor to empower and approve policies that advance stealth-schooling.

- *"As investment proceeds, the level of commitment to the policy becomes the status quo, and judgments are made relative to it"* (Jones, Thomas, & Wolfe, 2014, p. 153). School choice is the equivalent of a policy mantra in Indiana.

Blind faith in context and unquestioning allegiance to the free market allow leaders to sustain and approve judgments and decisions that have no value other than adherence to the marketplace status quo. Loyalty to privatization is such an ingrained part of some states' policy-making status quo that state leaders make decisions and judgments about school choice as an expression of this loyalty and without data or other student-centered outcomes for justification.

Indiana's allegiance to free market theory earned the state a grade of "A" from ALEC for its policies supporting charter schools despite the fact that charter schools throughout the state yield less than stellar academic results for students and despite the fact "that Indianapolis' charter schools are some of the city's most segregated" (Donheiser, 2017). Commitment at this level of intensity is both an overinvestment in, and a self-fulfilling prophecy for, the continuation of free market failures.

- *"Risk aversion"* [Jones, Thomas, & Wolfe, 2014, p. 153]. Overinvestment in privatization and encasing choice in a policy bubble are testimony to the risk-averse nature of free market thinking.

   Loath to forsake the comfort zone created by a policy bubble, free marketeers pour dollars, model bills, and political influence into nationwide efforts designed to ignore, avoid, or cover up the risks endemic to the market. Turning a blind eye to valid and reliable research about the deleterious effects for students of the context of privatization gives Indiana lawmakers carte blanche to commit to unexamined, unverified, untested ideology carried out through privatization legislation.

   Having created a policy bubble, privatization proponents throughout the nation avoid any risk that might burst the bubble. Persistent validation of policy that sustains and extends the free market status quo establishes risk avoidance as its own policy bubble.

Overinvestment establishes conditions that cover over the failings of the free market. Context is trumpeted as the end in mind of choice schooling. Policy invested in mechanisms and the perpetuation of mechanisms despite the costs becomes a substantial impediment to the purpose and quality of traditional public education.

The policy bubble surrounding context of free market schooling prevents traditional public education from accessing the statutory and funding power required to implement purpose and quality. Traditional public educators are left to pursue the rabbits set loose across the American landscape by model bills and other policy contrivances unleashed by free marketeers.

Chasing the Rabbits of Context

Most traditional public educators know the phrase "We're chasing the next rabbit." This phrase refers to the pointless and wasted professional energies devoted to programs, materials, policies, mandates, or other impositions designed to solve a problem du jour often linked to overinvestment in privatization.

Among other rabbits, colleagues chase privatization agenda items including standardized tests, ever-changing state and national curriculum standards, and multiple regulations attached to teacher quality. Changing direction almost yearly, without a coherent purpose in mind beyond an assortment of silver-bullet solutions wrapped in context, these ramifications of overinvestment leave too many colleagues, schools, and school districts focused only on the chase.

There is another phrase well known among educators: "This too shall pass." Often uttered in response to the mandates, requirements, and changes associated with chasing the latest rabbit, this dismissive, discouraged response is often the only rejoinder of traditional public education colleagues as they go through the motions of rabbit chasing.

Colleagues lose sight of the primary purpose of traditional public education when it's obscured by chasing both context and bubbles. The contextual emphasis of federal, state, local, and/or vendor expectations mangle professional practice in a tangle of conflicting objectives, goals, and purposes. Professional practice derails because "rabbit chasing" becomes the mandate instead of student learning.

The proposition offered here is that students prosper when *how to think* is the sought-after outcome of professional practice unfettered by context of the free market created by ancillary, discursive, and counterproductive legislative and ideological intrusions.

Traditional public educators deserve to be empowered to conquer important learning difficulties such as reading below grade level, math phobia, writing insufficiencies, or marginalization issues without being stymied by the teaching and learning dead end that is the context of free market schooling. The mistakes of context-centric inertia can be avoided because traditional public educators understand the central role of function in the pursuit of our primary purpose.

Educational Function and Professional Practice

Instead of reacting to rabbits and perseverating over zig-zagging contextual mandates as ends unto themselves, traditional public colleagues serve all students most effectively via a laser-like focus on the very difficult work of crafting function for instruction and learning experiences that engage students in the journey toward *how to think*.

Subject area content, interdisciplinary content, and/or standards can be woven within these learning experiences. The heartbeat of quality instruction, however, is not defined by content. Rather, function in traditional public education is expressed by pursuit of the primary purpose of traditional public education when quality instruction engages students with learning experiences in which habits of mind are learned, practiced, and/or applied.

Cognitive agency and successful intelligence are woven into student outcomes because function in traditional public education is not cluttered with the insubstantial glitter of the latest program, the sideshow of ideology, or pursuit that disconnects professional practices from engagement with *how to think*.

MORPHING BEYOND CONTEXT

How to stop chasing rabbits? How do colleagues ensure that a focus on a primary purpose is sustained? How to avoid the pitfall of context as an end unto itself? How do traditional public educators establish function using structure in any traditional public school? We suggest a simple answer to these questions: morph!

When we talk about morphing, we connect continuous improvement of our professional practice with the *theory of morphogenesis*.

Essentially, the theory of morphogenesis illuminates a synergy between our professional practice and educational institutions that traditional public education colleagues understand very well: "action and structure influence each other, but in alternating cycles over time" (Poole & Van de Ven, 1989, p. 573). The practical side of this theory boils down to realizing that the structures of our traditional public schools and our actions within these structures have an ongoing relationship.

When colleagues pay attention to the ebb and flow of structure with professional action, the theory of morphogenesis suggests that educators can gauge cycles of influence between these two so that function (engagement in instructional action to realize the purposeful student outcomes within *how to think*) improves and matures.

Morphing: Phase One

There are three segments or phases of this theory. The initial phase occurs when structure dominates behavior, the second phase is when individual actions and behaviors can change the structure, and a final phase occurs when these changes in structure are institutionalized (Poole & Van de Ven, 1989).

Thinking about the first phase, a school or school district structure can be understood in one of two ways when professional practice leads out teaching and learning to the primary purpose of traditional public education: either structure for professional practice is fully engaged with continuous improvement on the journey toward *how to think*, or structure for professional practice is not overtly focused on this journey.

If structure for professional practice is already devoted to *how to think* for all students, discussions earlier in this primer about continuous improvement and engagement with social justice provide opportunities for colleagues to interrelate action and structure as illustrated in the second and third phases of this theory.

Morphing: Phases Two and Three

If, however, a school or school district structure does not yet fully support professional practices for the journey to *how to think*, this theory provides insight into how structure and action can be employed to morph beyond the status quo.

Tools that are often utilized by traditional public educators—strategic planning and paradigm shifting—can be called into play to analyze the nature of phase one, or the current structure of a school or district. Using these tools, colleagues can determine the state of the structure and how collaborative action can morph existing instructional and cognitive behaviors to structure that supports the primary purpose of traditional public education.

The second phase of the theory of morphogenesis suggests a means to establish—in quality instruction aligned with *how to think* and provided during staff development—improvements as the strategic paradigm shift in the structure of a school or school district.

Using existing best practices—model-of instruction—and planning actions that implement improved quality of instruction—model-for instruction—colleagues act to create this shift by implementing quality instructional tactics to morph structure. This change establishes the third phase where structure becomes a focus on *how to think* and this focus includes the sustained development of this morphed structure via continuous improvement.

An understanding of the relationship between structure and action in traditional public education develops out of experiences with the learning outcomes attained when colleagues undertake educational practices aligned with our primary purpose.

The ongoing relationship between action and structure across the three phases of this theory within educational structure suggests the value of this primer as a resource from which colleagues can adopt and adapt information to improve school focus on *how to think*. There is tremendous power in the professional practice of traditional public educators that teaches *how to think*. This power is multiplied when educators understand and use these actions to influence structure in our profession for the ultimate benefit of our students.

MORPHING INTO FUNCTION AS INSTRUCTIONAL MAPPING

Function is a key difference between traditional public education and free market schooling. Function is the array of professional practices chosen by traditional public educators that constitute action in relationship with structure whereby continuous improvement of teaching and learning has

Instructional Mapping

Function is the conjunction of educators' creative processing with metacognitive knowledge where the successful intelligence of professional practice crafts quality thinking, teaching, and learning. As such, the numerous concepts, strategies, and theories presented in this primer are elements in the confluence of creative processing and metacognitive knowledge so that function can be understood as *instructional mapping*.

Instructional mapping is perhaps a misnomer because it is not the same as the mapping of a curriculum. Instructional mapping is responsive. A GPPS (Guided Professional Practice Selections), for instance, is used to orient decision-making about cognitive behaviors in response to student learning as it occurs in a classroom, lab, or other learning-scape.

In other words, function in traditional public education is the comprehensive teaching response that happens once the a priori plan of a curriculum map becomes professional behavior or action. Function is the professional response to the interactions of and the journey toward *how to think*. The conjunction of scholarship and practice that animates this discussion teaches that attention must be paid to function as the animated schematic of quality teaching and learning.

REPRISE: Meaning-Making within Function

Knowledge about thinking continues to develop. Professional practice in medicine and education continues to grow the realm of knowledge about human cognition. With understanding in the background, it's extremely important to quality instruction that what is known about thinking is included within function.

Thinking and meaning-making are points of practice that incorporate and develop the interplay of cognitive behaviors always present during teaching and learning. A focus on these two points of practice reveals the conjunction between the two dimensions in the revision of Bloom's Taxonomy—knowledge dimension and cognitive process dimension (Krathwohl, 2002)—and makes sense in a consideration of how best to engage students on the journey toward *how to think*.

Incorporating Kegan's theory of meaning-making into quality instruction gives insight into how to choose cognitive behaviors that advance the meaning-making during instruction. This aspect of function invites educators to lead out student meaning-making and natural thinking through habits of mind that are identified within a curriculum map. The tactics or strategies that engage our students with these habits of mind are, in part, oriented by an understanding and application of transformative learning theory.

REPRISE: Adopted Definitions within Function

To fulfill function in comprehensive traditional public education, it's necessary to orient quality instruction with definitions of both thinking and learning. These two definitions are points of practice because teaching and learning must be oriented by a clear understanding of both.

Categories of thinking and intelligence organize an educator's responses during instruction and they facilitate an evaluation of student learning. Teaching for, and watching for, analytic, creative, and practical intelligence as they segue with fluid thinking and/or crystallized thinking is where quality instruction can move students forward cognitively with selected habits of mind toward responsive cognition.

Quality instruction intends cognitive growth across developmental stages. So, working from definitions of thinking and learning permits instructional responses dedicated to growth, for instance, from concrete operations to early formal operations.

REPRISE: Responsive Cognition within Function

The journey to *how to think* passes through responsive cognition and cognitive agency. Emerging via instruction that fosters the interplay of habits of mind and layers of cognition, responsive cognition is the capacity for *how to think*. Emerging in action or in behaviors that seek a goal, responsive cognition is the precursor to cognitive agency.

Quality of thought evidenced in responsive cognition—an active blend of higher-order cognition, analysis, evaluation, and/or creativity—can be valuable unto itself. When responsive cognition fosters overt behavior aligned with societal orientation or principled orientation, function takes learning to a new level.

How to think is expressed out of the dialectic between formal operations and metacognitive knowledge. This synthesis, *cognitive agency*, is the cognitive state of affairs where choices, decisions, and behaviors strike a balance between individual and public goods bolstered by mediated identity and social justice.

DOWN IN THE SINKHOLE WITH PRIVATIZATION PROPONENTS

Free market schooling collapses into its context when its truncated, minimalist view of professional practice and quality instruction gives way. Marketeers view context—charter schools, vouchers, tax credits, and the like—as immutable. But, context of free market schooling collapses because mechanisms do not offer function that seeks purpose and establishes quality of teaching and learning. The policy bubble created on behalf of free market schooling is not strong enough to support the weight of quality education.

Mechanisms cause teaching and learning inertia; privatization proponents affix stealth-schooling to the permanence of ideology. This reliance on context forsakes structure, action, points of practice, continuous improvement, and function. The mistake riveted to the ideology of the free market is that context is static, promising nothing more than risk aversion, my-bias thinking, self-aggrandizement, and the fallacies of foolishness.

By contrast, structure and action of traditional public education have a mutual relationship within function; school and colleague engagement prompts a persistent cycle of improvement where traditional public education as a structure can morph as "both the medium and outcome of action" (Poole & Van de Ven, 1989, p. 574).

Bringing balance between individual and public goods reflects the dynamic of function in traditional public education where "structure and action coexist in a mutual process of production and reproduction. Action draws on structure; structure only exists in action; and they connect in modalities of structuration" (Poole & Van de Ven, 1989, p. 575). Traditional public educators incorporate continuous improvement as a modality of structuration that drives the student-centric focus of function.

WHAT TRADITIONAL PUBLIC EDUCATORS CAN DO: STRENGTHEN FUNCTION!

The free market and its adherents envision a contextual monster devouring tax dollars, destroying family values, and restricting individual freedom. Tunnel vision created by context ensures that free market adherents cannot see that choice schooling is fundamentally unstable, precariously gap-ridden, and poised over an unseen abyss.

When traditional public educators employ knowledge and cognitive process to establish educational function, free market schooling advocates go on the defensive. The student-centric role of function, and its outcomes in traditional public education, stand in sharp contrast to the ephemeral nature of free market theory, the sinkhole of its context, and the policy bubble around it.

- *Traditional public school educators* understand the value-added nature of balance between individual and public goods for U.S. democracy, but proponents of privatization have no vocabulary and no practices that speak to a better future for all students. The power of *how to think* established for a future of choices for all students by traditional public education is pushed away in favor of marketplace mechanisms.

The blatant abandonment of quality instruction and higher-order learning and reliance on context leaves free market proponents without a way to define the characteristics of a good school beyond reference to mechanisms and mindless repetition of the outcomes that "might be" and "may be" (Loeb, Valant, & Kasman, 2011, pp. 145–146).

Dialogue with policy-makers about function, purpose, and quality demands strong listening skills, patience, and data. Traditional public educators should use the structure of traditional public education and the broken promises of the free market to burst the policy bubble surrounding choice schooling.

- *Difficulty measuring* the connections between instruments and outcomes in privatization (demonstrated by a persistent absence of data indicating that stealth-schooling has a relationship with academic proficiency) is no impediment to the zest of ideologues for their bubble.

This see-no-evil approach by free market enthusiasts suggests that if traditional public education colleagues engage in dialogue with policy-makers with information about the disconnection between state testing and *how to think*, an opportunity is created.

Opening the eyes of stakeholders by demonstrating that overinvestment in policy for the free market is fundamentally flawed provides an especially effective way to engage multiple voices in communications with legislators and other leaders.

Speaking to policy-makers about a state's economic health by revealing the damage done by the free market policy bubble establishes another data-based connection that can and must be made. And, when marketplace adherents claim that choice schooling is effective, traditional public education colleagues and stakeholders must share data that no connection exists between free market schooling and any valid and reliable measure of academic excellence.

- *Traditional public school colleagues* should take advantage of cognitive dissonance among policy-makers when data and information about professional practices exposes the sinkhole of context beneath free market theory.

Cognitive dissonance, while it can evoke an initial emotional denial from policy-makers, has the potential to defuse emotion by deconstructing an existing level of commitment to the free market. Providing this perspective—and acknowledging that it constitutes cognitive dissonance for the policy-maker—about the value-added nature of traditional public education allows public educators to work with policy-makers to compare and contrast choice schooling (means, mechanisms, cost, overinvestment, bubble) with traditional public education (*how to think*, results, student focus).

The link between student success and professional practices becomes a generative, value-added, student-focused investment when traditional public education colleagues engage policy-makers with data that portends excellence for students, families, and society.

- *Providing information* about inefficiencies, fiscal hocus pocus, and academic failures that accompany free market schooling means that overinvestment becomes a topic with which traditional public educators should confront state leaders.

The bankrupt quality of market-based schooling and the significant costs of its policy bubble (portrayed via data from each state) should be researched by traditional public school allies as the centerpiece of forthright dialogue. The policy bubble deserves to be broken on behalf of the restoration of traditional public education and on behalf of a united state-wide effort to support the function and primary purpose of traditional public education.

- *Inform state legislators* and other leaders about the evaluative criteria used to assess overinvestment in the sinkhole of free market context. Again, the data that traditional education colleagues acquire about the failures of choice education must be incorporated into civil discourse.

This data and dialogue with policy-makers substantiates the validity of the evaluative criteria developed by Jones, Thomas, and Wolfe (2014). Calling into question the extent to which a policy bubble exemplifies the oxymorons and failures of privatization shines a spotlight on the multitudes of students negatively affected by the bubble.

This part of a civil confrontation should incorporate information about the extent to which privatization's sinkhole swallows up opportunity, funding, and futures for the overwhelming majority of students in a state.

- *Share improvements* in professional practice and student successes illuminated by examples of cognitive agency with policy-makers.

Demonstrate that traditional public education colleagues apply the phases of the theory of morphogenesis because our students must be prepared with successful intelligence to meet future challenges and opportunities. Evidence that professional practice excels at the task of strengthening student thinking, which in turn balances individual and public goods, should be used to indicate the value-added state of function in our profession.

The point of anchoring ideas with theory is to encourage and engage colleagues with the understanding that theory is a device for activating knowledge already possessed (Astley, 1985, p. 502). The theory of morphogenesis (as just one example of a theory that is useful to sustain and grow the quality of professional practice) gives insight into how actions and behaviors can cycle with what educators know about structure of traditional public education to improve function as a means toward the end in mind of traditional public education.

SEVEN

Free Market ATMs from Coast to Coast

The mechanisms of the free market require a significant transfusion of cash. Funding blossoms from a number of sources: state statutes, per-pupil state funding, legislative generosity, tax avoidance, tax credits, real estate gambits, and education savings plans are revenue streams at the micro level that nurture privatization with a concomitant negative effect on traditional public education (Mayer, 2017).

Information about funding and free market schooling begins with a stark reminder offered in the comment of one charter school principal in Detroit who shared a succinct statement about privatization in Michigan: "That's all it is now—it's moneymaking" (Binelli, 2017, p. 5).

THE ATM FOR FREE MARKET SCHOOLING IN THE STATES

It's important to realize that sizeable portions of the funding for privatization is allocated from state coffers.

Per-pupil Funding, Legislative Generosity, and Tax Avoidance

Free market schools, including those operated by for-profit corporations, receive a state's per-pupil funding allotment just as traditional public schools do. For instance, in Tennessee, the approval of a virtual school operated by K12, Inc. (one of the corporate members of ALEC) meant the corporation received the state's per-pupil payment of $5,300 for each student enrolled.

This $10.5 million annual payment to K12, Inc. resulted from an initial enrollment of two thousand students in this online school, most of whom were previously home-schooled students (Underwood & Mead, 2012). This sizeable payment added a fiscal commitment to the state budget that otherwise did not exist. Elsewhere, charter schools in Michigan receive close to $1 million annually in taxpayer funding (Jesse, 2014).

Annual state funding in Indiana for charter schools totals $300 million while payments for vouchers total an additional $150 million; these tax dollars otherwise would pay for traditional public education (Herron & Fittes, 2017). When early statewide voucher allocations in Indiana went unused, the unspent balance was not returned to traditional public schools. Further, the legislature eliminated special funding support put in place to help adjust special circumstances related to funding inequities among Indiana's public school districts.

Funding for traditional public schools in Indiana diminished rapidly once the diversion of funding to privatization programs began. An Indiana study (Boyland & Ellis, 2015) noted that as voucher distributions through the state budget increased, funding to traditional public schools through the state's foundation grants declined.

Indiana's per-pupil amount for traditional public schools in 2009 of $4,825 decreased to $4,280 per pupil by 2012. The reduction of per pupil funding in traditional public education, coupled with the elimination of additional support for school districts with declining enrollment, created significant overall reduction of funding for many Hoosier school districts (Boyland & Ellis, 2015).

More dollars for privatization and fewer dollars for traditional public education put an exclamation point beside the effect of free market thinking. Indiana's example, again, is instructive; on average in 2014, "Indiana charter schools received $7,080 per student while traditional public schools only received $6,415 per student" (Long, 2018, p. 35). Boyland and Ellis (2015) found that, since 2009, reductions in funding for Hoosier school districts meant that by 2012 average-sized school districts of 1,857 students suffered a loss of more than $1 million.

In 2013, an average-sized Indiana district experienced an additional funding loss of $790,000 (Boyland & Ellis, 2015). Across the nation, the extent and impact of less funding for traditional public education is captured in the fact that "schools in high poverty areas receive, on average, $5,500, or 29%, less per student than all other districts in the US" (Strauss, 2015).

The effect of declining dollars for traditional public education cannot be calculated simply by citing financing numbers. An analysis from the bipartisan Center for Budget and Tax Accountability indicated that "Indiana's voucher program may actually diminish student achievement in the state over time because it diverts public taxpayer dollars away from the state's public education systems" (Schneider, 2017, p. 4A).

It comes as no surprise to observers of traditional public education in Indiana, therefore, that during 2016 the effort of school districts to compensate for shortfalls meant that "40 percent of [traditional public] school districts were spending beyond their means, according to a legislative report" (Herron & Fittes, 2017, p. 6A).

Legislative Generosity

Funding from the allocation of per-pupil tax dollars does not capture completely the largesse that accrues to choice schooling from the state. Indiana's General Assembly provides an example of this phenomenon.

Generous support for privatization developed from the Hoosier legislature in the form of $50 million in low-interest loans to charter schools at the very end of one legislative session and in the form of additional legislative generosity that "forgave and paid off more than $90 million in charter school loans" (Cook & Turner, 2015). Neither of these fiscal outlays were made available in this form to traditional public education.

Corporate Tax Avoidance

Corporate tax avoidance is yet another means by which privatization adherents maximize cash flow from the state to benefit those who support their ideology. Murray and Murray (2010) identify several tactics used "by multi-state corporations to avoid paying their fair share of corporate income tax to your State" (Murray & Murray, 2010).

Passive Investment Companies, Real Estate Investment Trusts, Nexus Isolation, and Captive Insurance Companies are statutorily approved strategies by which large multi-state corporations (e.g., Walmart) avoid paying state taxes that fund public schools (Murray & Murray, 2010). Using these mechanisms between 1998 and 2001 Walmart avoided $350 million in corporate income taxes across twenty-seven states.

Tax Credits

Tax credits constitute funding magic for free market schooling on several levels. On one level, tax credits become revenue denied to the state that it would otherwise receive as a tax payment. In this case, although a voucher can be considered as tax dollars spent directly by the government, when marketeers pull tax credits out of their top hat to fund privatization, tax dollars do not reach the state. Tax credits are "lost" dollars to a state treasury because tax credit dollars are revenue that bypasses the state for the sole purpose of funding choice schooling (Carey, 2017; Fischer & Peters, 2016).

Tax credits are donations from individuals or corporations that fund what privatization proponents label, with a straight face, "scholarships." This mechanism "enabled lawmakers to work around state bans on the use of public funds to support religious institutions" (Brown, 2017). In

Indiana, this mechanism refunds 50 percent of any donor's gift to privatization schooling in the form of a state income tax credit.

Indiana is well prepared to provide this promised tax credit: $5 million was budgeted in 2009 for these neovouchers, and the amount allocated in 2017 skyrocketed to $26.5 million (Smith, 2017). In Florida, tax credits function so that "a corporation that owes $50,000 in Florida taxes, for example, could donate $50,000 and pay nothing to the state" (Brown, 2017).

Indiana's legislature legalized tax credits for private school tuition in a bill titled Scholarship Granting Organizations. Indiana's love affair with free market schooling leaves both democracy and the Hoosier electorate in the lurch when "the shell-game process of moving money from the public treasury to a donor to a nonprofit to a family to a private school makes it very difficult to account for how well those public dollars are ultimately spent" (Carey, 2017).

Tax credits are part of the negative funding spiral for traditional public education in the Hoosier state where "state education spending has not kept up with inflation, and still is not as high, in real dollars, as it was in 2011" (Brown & McLaren, 2016).

The tax credit game can lead to big financial victories for a select few. Savvy individuals and corporations can double their money when they live in states where it is possible to claim both the state's tuition tax credits and a federal deduction.

This combination results in "a risk-free, 100% profit of up to $4,500 per year for individuals or up to $100,000 for corporations" (AASA, 2017). The overall fiscal impact of tuition tax credits on traditional public education is clear: "seventeen states divert a total of over $1 billion per year toward private schools via school voucher tax credits" (AASA, 2017).

In too many instances these dollars are "beyond the purview of public accountability mechanisms" (Lubienski & Weitzel, 2008, p. 448). The fiscal "joke" played on traditional public education and all citizens reaches a zenith of sorts when for-profit management companies that operate choice schools invoke a classic example of chutzpah and "contend that the taxpayer money they receive to run a school is private, not subject to public disclosure" (Jesse, 2014).

Real Estate "Funding"

An unheralded but lucrative source of revenue for the benighted educational entrepreneurs who manage choice schools is found in real estate gambits unique to free market schooling. Examples abound of situations where choice school management organizations "buy buildings 'for a couple hundred thousand bucks, lease them to the choice school for a couple of years and then sell them' to the school 'for a few million'" (Binelli, 2017, p. 14). Management organizations often charge rent to the choice schools that they manage. Fourteen charter schools in Michigan, for instance, pay $1 million to National Heritage Academies, their Educational Management Organization (Binelli, 2017).

Impressive profits for financial institutions are available from sizeable tax breaks that accompany investment in choice schools located in so-called renewal communities (Binelli, 2017). Behind-the-scenes profit is yet another feature of privatization that has nothing to do with teaching, learning, or the future well-being of students but that has plenty to do with the lucrative fiscal chicanery practiced by free market schooling adherents.

Education Savings Plans

Ostensibly, saving for a worthy goal is a good thing. An education savings plan, as a result, gives the impression of putting away savings in advance to ensure payment for education later.

In several states across the nation, 529 Plans are mechanisms that allow tax-free savings to accumulate in anticipation of a family's payment of college tuition. Other plans, however, mangle the idea of saving for an educational future by siphoning public funding away from K–12 traditional public education to pay for private school tuition.

State-level plans that perform this function—known as Coverdell plans—are reflected in legislation proposed at the national level. One such example attempted to "create education savings accounts for military-connected students to pay for private school tuition and other education expenses" (Hefling, 2018b).

This attempt would have meant taking federal Impact Aid dollars—funding designed to offset the tax-exempt status of federal land located in traditional public school districts—away from public school districts to pay for private school enrollment of children of military families.

Multiple groups affiliated with the military, National Guard, and Reserves objected to this attempt because "the vast majority of the nation's nearly 600,000 school-age military children attend local public schools" (Hefling, 2018b). Despite the benefits for students in military families of attending traditional public schools, and despite the grassroots protests generated by military-affiliated organizations to thwart the end of Impact Aid funding, privatization proponents like the Heritage Foundation and almost three dozen additional advocates for choice schooling voiced support for the new proposal, which would provide a meager $2,500 of tuition support per student.

THE NATIONAL ATM FOR FREE MARKET SCHOOLING

Traditional public education colleagues not only tend to lack details about the origin and rationale that support free market theory but also fail to grasp the financial misdirection embedded in the theory.

Fortunately, writers who cover American education act as the proverbial canary in the coal mine and call attention accurately to free market advocates whose "motivation for dismantling the public education system—creating a system where schools do not provide for everyone—is ideological, and it is motivated by profit" (Underwood & Mead, 2012, p. 4).

Even without the largesse provided by state tax dollars, the sheer size of the cash machine available to fund the free market for education is daunting. When foundations (e.g., Americans for Prosperity), corporations (e.g., K12, Inc.), networks (e.g., ALEC), and/or choice school management companies actively promote privatization they "push a movement to divert public dollars from public schools and [that] undermines the public's confidence in our public schools" (Hefling, 2017, p. 6).

For instance, the Walton Family Foundation contributed more than $300 million to one out of every four charter school start-ups nationwide (Rich, 2014). The Walton Family Foundation also donated millions to efforts in New York City to dismantle teacher tenure, establish more rigid evaluation systems for teachers, and establish teacher performance pay (Rich, 2014).

Americans for Prosperity, the interconnected ideological juggernaut associated with Charles and David Koch, launched what they call the Libre Initiative (Hefling, 2017). Spending millions of dollars in eleven states, the Libre Initiative targets Hispanic families to build support for educational savings accounts "which enable families to use state tax dollars to pay for private school" (Hefling, 2017, p. 3).

Federal funding for choice schools is also in play; various budgetary initiatives are proposed regularly with dollars for charter schools hitting the $400 million mark (Leonor, 2018).

Playing Financial Hide-and-Seek

Additional organizations including the Center to Protect Patient Rights, Americans for Prosperity, the Bradley Foundation, the Mercer Foundation, DCI Group, and many others amass and distribute tens of millions of dollars in donations. Scholars have described the conglomeration of these free market proponents as a network of "think tanks, advocacy groups, trade associations, other foundations, and academic and legal programs" that receive and exchange untraceable funds in the form of donations to do the ideological bidding of the individuals and entities who contribute dollars to the cash machine for the free market (Mayer, 2017, p. 252–253).

The identities of individual, corporate, and foundation contributors and the precise amount of money donated from these sources are obscured within a thicket of tax-exempt foundations and other fiscal stratagems. In an elaborate game of financial hide-and-seek, donations to advance privatization are made to one entity, the entity receiving the original donation contributes that same amount to another networked entity which may, finally, give the money to advance stealth-schooling, or, may send the dollars through yet another identity-scrubbing foundation.

Chain donations like this occur to the point that the original source and amount of any given donation cannot be traced but the intent of the contribution can be fulfilled: privatization (Mayer, 2017).

Funding that is, essentially, laundered by this sophisticated networked national cash machine originates from allied donors and foundations at a "macro" level of privatization on behalf of free market theory to influence legislation and policy at a "micro" level in states across the country.

Money cleansed of association with its original donor ensures that legislative wheels are greased (with ALEC model bills; by lobbyists; via advertising; through all-expenses-paid junkets for legislators at ALEC conferences) at the micro level on behalf of the free market preferences of unidentified but wealthy individuals who likely do not live in and cannot vote in the state where the money has its impact.

WHAT TRADITIONAL PUBLIC EDUCATORS CAN DO: FOLLOW THE MONEY!

Free market theory generates a schooling boondoggle fueled by financing that benefits corporations, free market advocates, and well-heeled plutocrats. Absconding with dollars that should be spent for students in traditional public education, privatization proponents mock the public good and the value-added nature of a fully functioning democracy.

In the same way that most educators do not have information about the state and national ATMs that fund free market theory, most citizens, most parents/caregivers, do not have a clue about this funding. Providing information about free market financing and its impact on public schools has the potential for a meaningful impact. More than 60 percent of those responding to a prominent national poll, when given ample information, indicated opposition to using public funds to pay for private education (PDK, 2017).

Raising awareness about the free market's run on the bank of our future requires information to rally the support that traditional public education already enjoys, strategies that require no additional funding (obviously, because there is none), and actions that align with the primary professional purpose of traditional public education.

- *On the money trail!* All of America's children deserve an education adequate to their needs and adequate to the challenges and opportunities that the future will present to them. The misanthropic ideology that contradicts this fundamental premise of funding for traditional American public education, and the debilitating impact of the dollars diverted to support this ideology, should be broadcast widely among parents, caregivers, and citizens.

  Since free market schooling stipulates a de-funding of public education, the details about underfunding in each school district are a vital fact to share and share again.

  Local legislators and political leaders should be informed about the significant finding revealed in research that "states that send additional money to their lowest-income school districts see more academic improvement in those districts than states that don't" (Carey & Harris, 2016).

  The link between underfunding student learning and free market theory should be put in a spotlight. Parents, caregivers, and community members need to know when their tax dollars are not being used to support their child(ren). And, parents, caregivers, and citizens need to know that recent and significant research indicates that tax dollars do make a difference in traditional public education when it comes to delivering the quality learning that children and young people deserve (Carey & Harris, 2016).

- *Get the facts!* Ask specific questions to get the facts about state dollars that are diverted from traditional public education. Check with local print journalists for their "take" on this problem. Then, ask state legislators questions based on the information you gather about this misdirected funding. Once this information is shared with parents, caregivers, colleagues, and citizens about the loss of state revenue, then educators should use the democratic process to ensure that the community collaborates to restore the money denied to students.

- *Use the RTS facts.* It's important to introduce the concept of RTS (Return to Students) and keep it in front of state leaders and policymakers. Communications with state legislators and state political leaders need to ask for precise numbers about state funding for charters and vouchers.

  Data about per-pupil funding (to determine the amount provided for choice schooling compared with the amount provided for traditional public education) must be requested and, then, compared with numbers provided from local journalists and other reliable public sources. Precise numbers are needed, also, about tax credits and tax avoidance. Then, with numbers in hand, communicate with the school community about dollars taken away from students.

Ask traditional public education advocates to communicate with leaders about the necessity for restoring and increasing dollars to educate students in traditional public education. Lost funding, funding from the state given to ineffective and inefficient stealth-schools, must be restored to traditional public education to ensure the futures of students, communities, the economy, and U.S. democracy.

- *Follow the money in a different direction!* Charter schools provide banks and hedge funds with strong profit potential. Legislators, charter school authorizers, and charter school leaders should be asked about profit, debt, loans, and other opportunities for fiscal misadventure embedded in a state's statutory homage to privatization.

Tax breaks that may accrue to financial institutions for investing in charters, combined with the knowledge vacuum that afflicts charter authorizers and charter school boards when it comes to financial acumen and standards, are factors that can accelerate profit rates for companies and fiscal malfeasance in choice schools and organizations (Binelli, 2017).

- *Share state and community details.* When the free market drains tax dollars away from public education, sometimes attention is paid by local or statewide journalists. State and local data are important since they illustrate the negative impact of stealth-schooling on local students.

When traditional public educators use local, verified data to share, up front, the damage done by privatization's fiscal malpractice, a door is opened for parents, caregivers, and citizens that permits taking the "next step" of insisting on redress of this situation with state legislators and other officials.

- *Explain fairness in relationship to public education.* Talking about fairness with state legislators and other officials—whether in person, by phone, or via written communication—gives a human face to the consequences of inadequate state funding for traditional public education. When it comes to the importance of state taxes devoted to students, illustrations from day-to-day teaching and learning that demonstrate how children are being shortchanged by privatization need to be shared.

- *Illustrate the real-world benefits of traditional public education.* The benefits of a comprehensive curriculum—including offerings in the performing and fine arts, vocational skills, business, family, and consumer sciences—and the benefits of a robust set of extra- and co-curricular offerings illustrate how comprehensive traditional public education enriches the thinking and lives of all students.

Further, illustrations of equity, social justice, academic achievement, and other student successes in traditional public education demonstrate the proverbial tip of the educational iceberg; imagine, state leaders, what traditional public education could achieve if fully funded?!

In addition, the responsibility of the state to provide a fully funded quality education in traditional public schools (common schools referred to in state constitutions are a baseline for equity and equality often ignored or bypassed during the rush to privatization [Long, 2018]) should not be short-circuited by funneling monetary support away from this choice to the privatization of schooling, which eviscerates the meaning of U.S. democracy.

- *Establish equity and equality as non-negotiables.* Within school district budgets, traditional public school colleagues have accurate data about the impact of declining revenue on the futures of our students. This data must be utilized to create an accurate and data-based picture for the school community and for legislators who serve the school community because lost funding signifies declining equity and equality in traditional public education (Herron & Fittes, 2017).

  Policy-makers need to be informed about the research-based benefits for students that accrue from adequate funding for traditional public education including "how long students stayed in school and how much they earned as adults" (Carey & Harris, 2016). Tragically, traditional public schools in low-income communities of referendum states have little recourse for recovery when dollars are siphoned away by free market mechanisms. Business office officials in school districts should take the lead and articulate how the community is short-changed by privatization.

Traditional public education is affected dramatically when funding is siphoned away to support implementation of free market theory. Sharing accurate information about the disastrous fiscal impact of privatization creates awareness about what cannot be accomplished.

Clear and accurate details that demonstrate the negative fiscal impact of privatization on students in each traditional public school give parents and caregivers opportunities to understand negative legislative or administrative actions at the state level. Traditional public education colleagues must talk about how students and teachers are hurt by funding shortfalls created by the decisions of legislators and others smitten with the false promises and inequities delivered in the free market.

WHEN STUDENTS PAY THE COST FOR THE FREE MARKET OF SCHOOLING

The cost of free market schooling is borne by students. The alleged benefits of choice schooling drown in a storm of social Darwinism. Further complications arise because choice promoted by free market schooling is nothing less than educational apartheid. The story told by free market schooling adherents neglects to reveal that choice is severely limited.

For example, privatization puts children at risk because "when students use vouchers to get into private school, they lose most of the protections of the federal Individuals With Disabilities Education Act" (Goldstein, 2017). This loss is compounded because students often give up the added protection of having a teacher who is specialized in teaching students with an IEP when they enroll in choice schools.

McKinney and Shaffer (2018) found in a study of voucher students in Indiana that only 22 percent of voucher schools offered any kind of instructional program for students with learning disabilities and only 21 percent of the teachers who were assigned to teach students with learning disabilities in these schools had any kind of special education certification.

Buried in choice are costs that exacerbate the damage done by funding for free market schooling. Segregation, anemic achievement, denial of the public good, and a host of additional inequities are costs borne, ultimately, by students. The paradox woven into privatization and the free market is that benign language—efficiency, freedom, rights—hides the baleful ethos of the free market and its restrictions for large cohorts of the U.S. population. The free market is a breeding ground for the antithesis of democracy.

EIGHT

The Public Good and Traditional Public Education

Just like other complex ideas, the public good does not submit to a singular definition (Hostetler, 2003). Regardless, the necessity for attending to the public good in U.S. democracy is fashioned from the understanding that "how governments determine what laws and regulations need to be in place depends, largely, on citizens actions in areas of their lives that sometimes involved choices about whether to assume personal costs for a collective good" (Bolsen, 2013, p. 1).

The relationship between traditional public education and the public good will be discussed in this chapter. This discussion will illustrate the essential connection between *how to think* and balance between individual and public goods. While traditional public education is being pushed out on a limb, the viability of democracy in the United States teeters because it depends on realizing the purpose of traditional public education.

In this chapter, a viable definition of the public good and an illumination of how points of practice develop high-level information-processing and successful intelligence will be presented. These outcomes of traditional public education emerge as assets in America's democracy and as a counter to the primacy of self-interest at the base of free market schooling.

U.S. DEMOCRACY, INDIVIDUALS, AND EDUCATION

If free market theory disconnects individuals from their responsibilities and obligations to create and maintain the public good, what happens to U.S. democracy? If what is known about the potential of traditional public education is lost, can the primacy of self-interest suffice for the good of the nation? If citizens and educators do not know about free market theory and its intents, what are the implications for all students in all schools?

One way to think about answers for these questions is to discuss how individuals understand and respond to democracy in the United States. At times, and particularly in times of crisis—war, natural disasters, local catastrophes—U.S. citizens make significant choices and pay life-changing personal costs on behalf of the public good. But the ongoing health of democracy in the United States cannot, and should not, be sustained only by costs paid in the form of heroic responses to crisis.

Moreover, because crisis is relatively infrequent, without citizens capable of and willing to pay costs during normal times that are associated with cognitive agency, wisdom, and successful intelligence, the field of choice—literally and figuratively—is left to cost- and covenant-averse proponents of privatization and the free market.

Citizenship behaviors mired in the limitations imposed by my-side bias and natural thinking truncate the relationship that ought to exist between a citizen and U.S. democracy, with a particularly devastating impact on our most democratic institutions with traditional public education at the forefront.

DOCUMENTING THE PUBLIC GOOD

The intended relationship between each citizen and democracy is, unto itself, a public good and is captured in some of the earliest documents in U.S. history. The Mayflower Compact, for instance, proclaims the necessity to "covenant and combine our selves together in a civil body politic, for our better ordering and preservation . . . for the general good of the Colony, unto which we promise all due submission and obedience" (Mayflower Compact, nd).

The preamble to the U.S. Constitution emphasizes a more perfect union as the apotheosis of the public good. The goals of this evolving public good enshrined in the Constitution include justice, domestic tranquility, the general welfare, and the blessings of liberty (Constitution of the United States, nd).

Although these and other formative documents convey covenant at the heart of American democracy and extol the characteristics of this public good, no national document spells out the federal exercise of traditional public education as a means toward these ends. Instead, each state takes on education because it is an un-enumerated right in the U.S. Constitution. Indiana's state constitution, for example, devotes Article 8 to a Common School System.

The relationship between the Hoosier state and public education is anchored in the state constitution by a call for the general diffusion of knowledge and learning, which is "essential to the preservation of a free government." Indiana's constitution—like many other state constitutions—further indicates that it is a duty of the state legislature to "provide, by law, for a general and uniform system of Common Schools, wherein tuition shall be without charge, and equally open to all" (Indiana Constitution, 1851).

Consistent with the responsibility of each state to deal with education, in Massachusetts Horace Mann wrote that the purpose of the first-in-the-nation public school system was to ensure that "every child born within its borders shall be enlightened" (Mann, 1839, p. 47). From the first days of our democracy and from the first days of education for the American public, the public good and *how to think* appear as comingled priorities. Traditional public education is nothing less than the cornerstone of democracy.

Traditional public education, unlike free market schooling, makes no distinctions among those students who can and cannot enroll. The enlightenment of every child, the preservation of a free government, and a general and uniform system of common schools have long been central elements in the equation of democracy in the United States. Traditional public education goes a step further on behalf of democracy and claims responsibility for citizenship education.

CITIZENSHIP AND TRADITIONAL PUBLIC EDUCATION

On the surface, U.S. citizenship in traditional public schools takes the form of displaying our national ensign in every classroom, teaching American history, and presenting patriotic class plays. In the hundreds of classrooms and traditional public schools where the authors have taught, supervised, and visited, the great strength of diversity in our nation of immigrants is commemorated with a display of the flags of the many nations from which student families emigrated.

Displays like these, and the very design of our nation's flag, symbolize the enduring meaning and value of *e pluribus unum*. Beyond mere display, however, is behavior of students and staff in traditional public education: a dedication to our democracy and the patriotism embedded in the daily recitation of the Pledge of Allegiance to the United States of America. Outward demonstrations of citizenship and patriotism are, however, just the baseline for citizenship education in traditional public education.

The complexity of citizenship education and the dedication of traditional public schools to this subject are reflected in the fact that social studies education has long defined itself as citizenship education.

Furthermore, the value of citizenship education in traditional public education extends beyond the four walls of school because citizenship is "the fundamental institution that connects the individual bearer of rights to the protective agencies of the state. The civic realm of the state provides the main channels through which individuals can participate politically and share in governance (Kulsmeyer, 1996, p. 97)" (Patrick, 1999, p. 2).

There is a necessary presumption that citizenship depends upon individuals who have the cognitive wherewithal to choose the cost of citizenship for participation in governance for U.S. democracy. Sharing in governance requires a level of cognition whereby individuals exercise cognitive agency and choose to accept personal cost for a balance between individual and public goods.

Citizenship, in this way, is an example of successful intelligence because balancing the benefits of individual rights with the public good in a democracy cannot happen in an educational vacuum.

Your Nose and My Nose: Individual Freedom and the Public Good

Thinking is the transformation of mental representations of knowledge. To lead out from the restrictions of natural thinking via quality professional practice in traditional public education, these "manipulations must be systemic transformations governed by certain constraints" (Holyoak & Morrison, 2005, p. 2).

For traditional public education colleagues, these constraints are represented in costs connected with nothing less than the primary expectation of American democracy: balance between individual freedom and the public good.

Put in practical if metaphoric terms, balance connected with *how to think* invokes the cost of a reliable democracy. Traditional public education evidences this constraint, the required personal cost, as payment required for the public good in U.S. democracy: constraint of a person's right to swing his/her individual needs into the nose of covenant.

DEFINING THE PUBLIC GOOD

Symbiosis between individual rights and successful intelligence crafts a one-for-all-and-all-for-one ethos in U.S. democracy. Here lies the balance in the achievement of the public good as "things that benefit everyone but which no one has an individual incentive to provide" (Bolsen, 2013, p. 1).

This sense of covenant, of achieving the qualities necessary for a more perfect union, establishes equality as a non-negotiable of U.S. democracy where "a public good is something that cannot feasibly be withheld from others in a group if it is provided for any member of that group (Olson 1965)" (Bolsen, 2013, p. 2).

The public good arises from the wisdom that an individual's right to swing his/her arm ends where the nose of another person begins. This example is often associated with the unwritten social contract that exists when individuals choose to pay a cost—forswearing unlimited arm-swinging—to garner the benefit of not being punched in the nose. In a less allegorical example, the personal constraint represented by the cost of paying taxes yields the public goods represented by first responders, public utilities, public governance, public infrastructure, public libraries, and traditional public education.

These are, of course, the tangible public goods that individuals cannot provide on their own. Less tangible, but more fundamental to the nature of U.S. democracy are the costs embedded in quintessentially American bedrock: liberty, justice for all, and equality for all.

When American citizens have the cognitive capacity necessary to choose to pay the price associated with these intangible benefits, the cognitive and overt behaviors that underlie equality, social justice, and enlightened self-interest are possible. Payment—a great cost for choice education proponents but a welcome "freebie" for traditional public educators—to reach this end in mind includes the forfeiture of my-side bias and thinking-as-restriction.

For free market advocates, this is too great a cost because the price to acquire the public good means giving up the primacy of self-interest lying at the core of privatization. The primary expectation of democracy in the United States, and the only constraint of significance at its core (the balance between individual and public goods), are costs that marketeers will not pay. Privatization proponents refuse to invest when traditional public education fulfills its primary purpose to teach students *how*—not what—*to think* (Sternberg, Reznitskaya, & Jarvin, 2007).

Without traditional public education, without the growth of individual cognitive behaviors necessary and sufficient to citizenship and choosing the cost of democracy, the public good expires. The original spark for taking our nation beyond the primacy of self-interest embodied by privatization was taxation without representation. Ending this specific example of tyranny of the few over the many established a fundamental premise upon which the United States was founded in the blood of our forefathers.

Yet, the gains represented by this sacrifice have been usurped in many states more than two hundred years later through the work of billionaires who no longer carry inclusive concepts in their net of value. Privatization proponents, for instance, override the representative democracy of local traditional public schools. Here, governance historically is embodied in local representation from the community (taxation with representation stops tea parties!) in the form of the school board for a school district.

But this most immediate, community-embedded form of representation disappears when—with Indiana leading the way once more—legislators (during the 2018 legislative session) threw out the boat with the tea and replaced the community's authority to elect local patrons with appointed board members who usurp school community governance to govern free market choice schools (AP, 2018).

As they upend local governance and while they reestablish taxation without representation to support the free market, proponents ensure that students experience only macro-level platitudes about the foundations of our democracy. Without models-of about participation in local governance, and in the absence of examples that link macro and micro levels of engagement in democracy, the disappearance of local representation and the exercise of cost without local control symbolizes the effect of free market schooling on democracy: disconnection, misrepresentation, and absentee governance.

REPRISE — Cognitive Agency

The agency necessary for the success of our democracy—which includes giving "voice" to covenant woven into the foundations of democracy and captured by participation in a variety of local governance opportunities—emerges from teaching and learning galvanized to points of practice in traditional public education.

Meaning-making, natural thinking, and personal assets of each student are baseline elements of every person's cognitive capacity. Transformative definitions of thinking and learning advance instruction that interweaves habits of mind in accord with the development of each student to engender responsive cognition.

Responsive cognition is the dialogical interplay of habits of mind by an individual using "multiple frames of reference to generate and deliberate about various perspectives on the issue at hand" (Sternberg, Reznitskaya, & Jarvin, 2007, p. 152). From this cognitive conjunction, agency behavior emerges.

Specifically, responsive cognition is the interplay of habits of mind and layers of cognition in the human brain that establishes each student's capacity for cognitive agency. Cognitive agency is the capacity to choose and act to balance behaviors that benefit both the good of the individual and the public good.

The primary purpose of traditional public education recognizes that "thinking as an autonomous and responsible agent is essential for full citizenship in democracy and for moral decision making in situations of rapid change" (Mezirow, 1997, p. 7). Cognitive agency is necessary for U.S. citizens to be able to choose to pay the price of abandoning my-side bias and accept the constraints symbolized by the social contract.

REPRISE — Wisdom

When students evidence cognitive agency, wisdom is facilitated. Wisdom is another complex concept that has no singular definition. The definition that most meaningfully illustrates wisdom as the conjunction of cognitive agency with human development is offered by Sternberg et al. (2007):

> The application of intelligence, creativity, and knowledge as mediated by values toward the achievement of a common good through a *balance* among (a) intrapersonal, (b) interpersonal, and (c) extrapersonal interests, over the (a) short- and (b) long-terms, in order to achieve a balance among (a) adaptation to existing environments, (b) shaping of existing environments, and (c) selection of new environments. (p. 145)

To understand wisdom in this way suggests the value of the dynamic of professional practice where natural thinking, student assets, meaning-making, responsive cognition, and cognitive agency — and their attendant characteristics and behaviors — enter a dialectic with interests/environment and lived experience of each student. Defining wisdom in this way opens a door to realizing that instructional choices must adapt, shape, and select professional practice environments in function of traditional public education that is best suited to the pursuit of our primary purpose.

Defining wisdom in this way calls attention to the formative nature of covenant. The common or public good presupposes that learners have a secure base that is "the attachments that form you and the things you then do for yourself" (Brooks, 2017). When the things that people do for themselves are crafted by *how to think*, wisdom exists that can validate attachments including the covenant of balance between individual and public goods.

COMPREHENSIVE PUBLIC EDUCATION IN THE REAL WORLD

A moving and tragic example of this level of wisdom crafted by teaching and learning experiences in comprehensive traditional public education occurred after the horrific massacre at Marjory Stoneman Douglas High School in Parkland, Florida, during 2018. Survivors of the shooting that killed seventeen students and faculty applied the breadth and depth of their learning to engage the nation in short- and long-term analysis of gun violence.

Responsive cognition and cognitive agency were reflected in the wisdom of statements made and the successful intelligence in actions taken by students in the aftermath of tragedy to shape existing environments and select new environments.

What students from this comprehensive traditional public high school learned — including required classes in public speaking, a robust fine arts/

drama program, and extensive print and electronic journalism options—yielded successful intelligence, wisdom, in the form of "skills beyond standardized testing and rankings [that created] passionate citizens who are spring-loaded for citizenship" (Lithwick, 2018).

Comprehensive traditional public education fosters outcomes of a transformative nature. The problem, however, is that the equitable pursuit of *how to think* is denied across the nation and throughout traditional public education because free market schooling siphons away funding, supportive legislation, and academic focus.

The gist of the incredible demonstration of successful intelligence under the most difficult circumstances by the students at Marjory Stoneman Douglas High School is that it represents what ought to be about cognitive behaviors, successful intelligence, and citizenship. Unfortunately, the devastating impact of the ideologues pushing the free market means that "the story of Marjory Stoneman Douglas students is a story about the benefits of being a relatively wealthy school district at a moment in which public education is being vivisected without remorse or mercy" (Lithwick, 2018).

The successful intelligence, successful citizenship, and wisdom represented in the cognitive behaviors and actions of students from comprehensive traditional public education are outcomes of enduring value to our democracy. In this case, successful intelligence laden with data and details devoted to ending gun violence entailed a daunting cost for Stoneman Douglas High School students.

When they shared their ideas and citizenship engagement, students were subjected to defamation, conspiracy mongering, and hate speech from social media participants, television personalities, and politicians.

Reaching the destination of *how to think* does not ensure any individual conflict-free engagement with and for U.S. democracy. Sometimes, the outcomes that attend *how to think* entail costs of their own. Despite this, the empowered students at Stoneman Douglas High School, who initiated dialogue infused with habits of mind to establish new environments of greater safety for all, persisted.

How to think demonstrated by students from Marjory Stoneman Douglas speaks to the intentions and merits of the outcomes lost without support for traditional public education to serve the public of our democracy.

Stitzlein (2017) identifies five defining characteristics of a true public school. True public schools welcome all students; prepare active citizens; respond to the public; cultivate dialogue that is tolerant; and sustain citizenship participation. A true public school was mirrored in the cognitive and overt behaviors of student survivors of the shooting at Stoneman Douglas.

Traditional public education colleagues' professional practices lead out to successful intelligence and successful citizenship. But, without knowing that free market theory proponents push these outcomes away and replace them with the primacy of self-interest, traditional public educators in the United States risk a clueless response, or no response at all, that leaves students and U.S. democracy stranded.

REPRISE — Successful Intelligence

Reflecting the intermittent growth and expression of covenant through U.S. history, traditional public education offers the forum to learn what it takes for citizenship in democracy. *How to think* empowers individuals to choose balance via cognitive agency. Wisdom emerges in the conjunction of cognitive agency and human development.

Traditional Public Education and Social Justice Precepts

Successful intelligence emerges from the dialectic between wisdom and the fundamental social justice precepts of U.S. democracy. From this dialectic comes the synthesis of choices and decisions that signify an individual's capacity to choose to bear the cost of the forfeiture of my-side bias and the primacy of self-interest that infects the free market.

This exercise of balance inherent in the primary purpose of traditional public education fulfills the government's interest in social cohesion in a democracy (Levin, 2002). Successful intelligence fulfills individual interests with participation in governance whereby the environment of democracy creates benefits within the balance of individual and public goods.

The nature of this social cohesion for the unique qualities of American democracy is vouchsafed only when citizens learn *how to think*. Successful intelligence is the array of behaviors that engage individual capacities of cognitive agency for balance. "Successfully intelligent people adapt to, shape, and select environments" (Sternberg & Grigorenko, 2004, p. 274).

Democracy and Education: Environments of the Public Good

The imperative of the pursuit of *how to think*, then, is to ensure "students can learn to search for and then try to reach the common good—a good where everyone wins and not only those with whom one identifies" (Sternberg, Reznitskaya, & Jarvin, 2007, p. 148). Reaching the common good emerges in cognitive agency, wisdom, and successful intelligence.

When the primary purpose of traditional public education is pursued, the interweaving of habits of mind (responsive cognition) facilitates, ultimately, the balancing of goods (successful intelligence) in a functioning democracy to foster sustained realization of justice for all within the sociocultural context of U.S. democracy (cognitive agency). To exercise a balance between individual rights and the public good is difficult in the free market and for its proponents because natural thinking and meaning-making are out of balance, tilted toward self-interest.

Cognitive agency and wisdom are necessary if behaviors of social justice symbolized in sociocultural intentions such as "one from many" or "liberty and justice for all" are to be manifest in the successful intelligence that creates day-to-day U.S. democracy (Kahlenberg & Potter, 2014). The pursuit of *how to think* in traditional public education is the precursor required for successful democracy.

WHAT TRADITIONAL PUBLIC EDUCATORS CAN DO: PLAN AND CREATE MOSAICS!

An understanding of cognitive agency, wisdom, and successful intelligence establishes a connection with the breadth of behaviors that are the enduring objectives of quality instruction in traditional public education. The professional practices chosen to craft the mosaic of quality instruction valorize all students' experiences by applying knowledge and cognitive behaviors in environments where citizenship and social justice are nurtured.

These professional practices constitute a bulwark against the theory of the free market because both individual goods and the public good are served. Free market theory fails to serve all students and thereby fails to serve U.S. democracy. Understanding gives traditional public school educators opportunities for meaningful responses based on the information in this primer.

- *Teach supportive cognition.* Quality instruction engages each student with knowledge, memory, and habits of mind to interplay as responsive cognition. To construct responsive cognition over time means that lessons should incorporate direct instruction (accomplished during focus lessons) about these thinking behaviors and agency skills.

  Supportive cognition is both the habits of mind necessary to acquire more complex cognition and the self-talk of a learner that expresses high confidence in the personal ability to make these ongoing acquisitions. The nature of supportive cognition and the quality instruction that teaches it are shared by several authors (Schmoker, 2006; Marzano, 2007; Brown, Roediger, & McDaniel, 2014) but lie beyond the scope of this narrative.

- *Big questions!* Mysteries, unknowns, problems, cognitive dissonance—all inspire learning. The human tendency to make sense of things, to adapt, to make meaning, to understand how and why, are resources of intrinsic value to quality instruction. Creating lessons centered around a big question requires the application of habits of mind. Big questions provide a constant reminder about not only the task at hand but why the task is worth doing.

Big questions (across a variety of subjects) can sound like this: How could World War II have been prevented? What would you write to describe how to calculate the square footage of our school building geometrically? What are the formative conclusions you draw from *Heart of Darkness* and how do you back each one up using the author's words? Which two pieces of music that we have studied this semester affect you emotionally and how do you explain this impact using the score?

- *Create quality instruction!* Quality instruction involves persistently teaching students that they have the capacities necessary to find answers for big questions when they apply habits of mind. And, quality instruction invokes students' capacities for not only previously taught cognitive behaviors but also connects contemporaneous units to new habits of mind that allow students to expand and apply their emerging capabilities for *how to think*.

  Calling forth prior knowledge about supportive cognition while adding new cognitive skills extends and challenges students into gathering new data, perspectives, and information. Interwoven, these are among elements of the foundation for seeking answers during classroom activities (e.g., a simulation, a debate, a mock trial, a mock conference, etc.) fostered by quality instruction.

- *Student wisdom.* Throughout quality instruction during applied learning experiences, students need opportunities to articulate by paraphrasing the cognitive behaviors that they're using. Learning about how to implement supportive cognition is an early step in quality instruction for student wisdom.

  Highlighting through direct instruction the habits of mind and cognitive capabilities that are "in play" during a lesson facilitates an increase of responsibility taking by students for reflecting upon their own cognition. Student articulations about the cognitive behaviors they utilize to establish and justify responses during learning activities further the pursuit of wisdom and envelop learners in knowledge and appreciation of their own capabilities.

U.S. DEMOCRACY, DIVERSITY, AND THE PUBLIC GOOD

All who serve in traditional U.S. public education know that each school, each classroom, is incredibly diverse and that this represents a great strength of U.S. society and a great opportunity for the profession.

Although diversity is a core strength of traditional public schools, U.S. history, at best, reflects an intermittent and incomplete development of rights, equity, social justice, and equality. These principles and their articulation are the evolving panorama of the American Dream, the realization of which is replete with fits, starts, setbacks, successes, conflicts, and glacial progress.

Over time, the United States lurches toward giving more than lip service to the meaning of justice for all. American history—Reconstruction (which broached an initial and "an unprecedented commitment to the ideal of a national citizenship whose equal rights belonged to all Americans regardless of race" [Foner, 1990]); the Progressive Era; Women's Suffrage; the labor movement; the Civil Rights Movement; school desegregation; the Farm Workers movement; the LGBTQ rights movement; the MeToo movement; innumerable individual struggles for justice and equality—is the story of the national struggle to realize the promises of covenant and equality in the American Dream imagined in the noble words of U.S. foundational documents.

Traditional public education is very much a part of this bumpy ride. Traditional public education did not even exist until decades after the beginning of our republic. Professional practice has not always nurtured social justice and has not always pursued *how to think* for all students.

A Bumpy Educational Journey

Numerous state statutes during U.S. history, and recent additions like the mechanisms of privatization, stand in the way of equity and equality in schools throughout the nation. National initiatives (often federal statute or judicial action [e.g., *Brown v. Board*, 1954]) slowly develop to the point that justice for all in American schools begins to include national origin, religious, racial, disability, and/or gender diversities.

This recognition and the diversities of our students evolved the role of traditional public education as the crucible of emerging equity and equality in our democracy. With time, traditional public education became our nation's most prominent civic institution where, to paraphrase Robert Frost's depiction of home, when you showed up, they had to let you in (Frost, 1942).

Despite, and sometimes because of, this fitful, often difficult, professional history (Goldstein, 2015), legions of traditional public education colleagues embrace "a view that says important progress can be made from the (imperfect) conditions in which we find ourselves" (Hostetler, 2003, p. 353). After all, it is in the nature of learning and education to improve whatever the current conditions may be.

The story of the United States with our traditional public schools alongside is about growing, gradually, painfully, greater than the original eighteenth-century limits embedded in "all *men* are created equal" and into ever more complete, just, and equitable public implementation of a more perfect union in legal, social, and behavioral terms. Although traditional public education has no legal mandate from the federal government to change or improve the nation's development of liberty and justice for all, it is the function of traditional public education as envisioned in state constitutions to develop the individual's capacity to do so.

In this way, the relationship between traditional public education and U.S. democracy evidences Vygotsky's zone of proximal development. The evolving maturity of our democracy, alongside the environments made new in traditional public education by *how to think*, constitute the synergy for the development of the public good.

The Public Good and Information Processing

The valuable impact of traditional public education on the relationship between citizens and American democracy is illustrated by knowledge about high-level and low-level information processing. Bolsen (2013) illustrates the degree to which responsive cognition and cognitive agency are integral to an individual's capacity for high-level information processing.

The capacity for high-level information processing is expressed when individuals "closely attend to information regarding appropriate norms (i.e., 'high-level' processing)" (Bolsen, 2013, p. 5). The complex cognitive interplay that defines high-level processing allows students to analyze different options, to evaluate the worth of competing ideas, and to choose behaviors aligned with this process for meaning-making. *How to think* constitutes a platform essential to the capacity of individuals to identify norms appropriate to democracy, to the balance between individual and public goods.

Natural and my-side bias thinking evidence low-level information processing (Bolsen, 2013). Low-level processing is cognitive interplay where attending to information about appropriate norms yields behavior consistent with the bandwagon effect. "Bandwagon effects occur when people believe and do things merely because other people do it" (Bolsen, 2013, p. 5).

Low-level information processing, my-side bias thinking, and the bandwagon effect are nurtured by the code and impressions of privatization. The language of the free market plays to FUD (fear, uncertainty, doubt [Moyers, 2014]), which is invoked intentionally to unsettle parents/caregivers and depends upon impressions to influence an audience with two fallacies of foolishness: unrealistic optimism and omniscience.

Fostering these fallacies in combination with foisting stealth-schooling on the public at large enables the bandwagon effect as a force sufficient to rationalize privatization. Lest this comment appear as mere bluster and bombast, one of the three authors served as a private school teacher and administrator for the first seventeen years of his career and watched omniscience ride by on the bandwagon of stealth-schooling:

I cannot count the number of times I heard the rhetorical assertion, "public school teachers are in it for the money" or "public school educators are all atheists or agnostics intent on destroying the souls of our children." Imagine the pleasant surprise I experienced when, becoming principal for the first time in a public, urban, elementary school, I discovered that a great number of the teachers attended the same church I did and even taught Sunday School or worked in the church nursery. What I found was that the most dedicated teachers with whom I ever worked were in traditional public schools. They often gave of their own limited resources; they provided food for students on the weekends after the children were discovered digging in the school dumpster over the weekend for food to take home. The level of dedication and passion I observed was unmatched by anything I had ever seen or experienced in the private sector schools where I once worked. The dilemma, of course, is that the public hears that private is always better than public and that traditional public educators are grossly overpaid.

High-Level and Low-Level Information Processing

The difference between high- and low-level information processing is the capacity of an individual to develop and act upon meaning when norms are invoked. The primary purpose of traditional public education entails information processing that facilitates individual capacity to invoke norms—including those associated with democracy—as a key to choosing behavior on behalf of the public good (Bolsen, 2013).

But, forswearing data while relying on mythology, mechanisms roll off the ideological assembly line to deliver stealth-schooling across the United States. Stealth-schooling, in turn, delivers my-side bias thinking and imposes the fallacies of foolishness to the cognition of America's students. In the event of the complete destruction of traditional public education accompanied by the delimitation of equitable access to cognitive agency, wisdom, and successful intelligence by a free market, an assembly line to perpetuate low-level information processing moves forward to replace balance in U.S. democracy.

THE FREE MARKET IGNORES THE PUBLIC GOOD

Traditional public educators defend against a theory espousing thinking, behaviors, and embedded processing of norms antithetical to a primary purpose and to the cognitive behaviors necessary for successful democracy. Critics contend that the context of traditional public education is a bloated, inept bureaucracy (Chubb & Moe, 1990).

The cure proposed for this malady by critics is a free market where choice of schooling in and of itself substitutes for the cohesion central to democracy. As Mead (2016) indicates, absent from this dedication to "choice for choices' sake is any suggestion of the public school as a public good—as a centering locus for a community and as a shared pillar of the commonweal, in which all citizens have an investment."

Low-level information-processing evinced by the vouchers established in the wake of *Brown v. Board* (Goldstein, 2015; Levin, 2002) facilitated the negation of justice as a centering locus for covenant. For traditional public education colleagues, developing the capacity for high-level information processing means that students—the voting public of the future—can choose norms that bring balance. Our democracy and its education, as we know from Dewey (1916), are inclusive constructs.

To serve all students and colleagues and to serve all citizens, traditional public educators accept responsibility for educational sustainability defined as "the capacity of a system to engage in the complexities of continuous improvement consistent with deep values of human purpose (Fullan, 2005, p. 114)" (Leo & Wickenberg, 2013, p. 407). Eminent social studies educator John J. Patrick (1999) emphasizes this point:

> The people of a democratic country or nation-state may have various and overlapping identities based on such factors of society as religion, race, ethnicity, social class, and gender. However, the single identity possessed equally by all citizens of the polity, regardless of differences, is civic identity. (p. 2)

Civic identity, traditional public education, and the public good in U.S. democracy are inseparable. The public good embraced within traditional public education will always shine in the professionalism of a colleague of one of the authors, Mary Abbot.

TEACHER SNAPSHOT: MARY ABBOT

Mary Abbot was the embodiment of intelligence, courage, dignity, strength, compassion, persistence, and honor. She was an educator's educator. Her science classes wove classifying, using evidence, forming hypotheses, testing and evaluating hypotheses, and discussions into the lives of her students. Mrs. Abbot's professional career began in a segregated school where science equipment and textbooks, along with support for teachers who taught students how to think, were largely absent. Her retelling of those days sheds light on how instruction—even without the lab and experiment accoutrements of her subject area—engaged the assets her students brought to school with higher-order thinking that served as fuel for each student's future.

She spoke passionately, whenever we talked, about the successes her students attained as they grew up, graduated, and made their way into the world with intelligence, dignity, compassion. Mary spoke to her conviction that public education serves as the portal for students to access higher order thinking and the greater outcomes of democracy promised, but not yet delivered, to all. The public good created by Mary Abbot multiplied throughout the lives of her students.

Binoculars versus Spy Glass: A Clear View of Democracy

The opponents of traditional public education have no use for the public good because their monocular perspective is manifested only in the primacy of self-interest. Providing something of value to society, unless it involves increasing individual wealth, is counterproductive from the perspective of free market proponents. Free market theory does not speak to balance or covenant. Stealth-schooling does not invest openly in the cognitive behaviors required to advance something greater than the individual.

The public good of covenant enshrined in our nation's ethos has little value for proponents of mechanisms dedicated to imbalance. Adherents of free market schooling see the destruction of their own privileges in the statutory and regulatory initiatives and in social behaviors that broaden and improve social justice.

Those who would dismantle traditional public education emphasize the value of efficiency in a free market among the central concepts within their agenda: less government, preservation of individual wealth, and ideological purity. Free market adherents circle back on this logic when they contend that efficiency of choice creates efficiency of schooling because choosing establishes competition, which yields efficiency when parents and caregivers choose among schools and only the most efficient schools (which are the fittest) survive.

Little evidence exists that claims of efficiency made about choice schooling by free market proponents yield student performance relative to thinking/processing skills. On the contrary, privatization evidences low-level information processing, my-side bias thinking, and other manifestations of ideological purity divorced from *how to think*, cognitive agency, wisdom, and successful intelligence.

For privatization proponents, ideological purity is found in the free market where funding, policy, and politics operationalize ideological mechanisms, protect private wealth, and deconstruct government cost with a special emphasis on the deconstruction of traditional public education.

Stealth-schooling, the most obvious manifestation of ideological purity, grows in networks of profit centers, publicly funded religious education, and disparate individual enterprises. Instead of *how to think* and the cognition necessary to balance individual and public goods, these marketplace schools are all about foisting low-level information processing on decision-makers in unsuspecting families who are told privatization offers the "fittest" schooling.

This is free market theory at its most egregious because the outcomes of greatest value constitute a best fit with the self-identified needs of a wealthy, self-indulgent cohort in U.S. society. The purpose of the free market is cost abatement that increases wealth for adherents while regulation, government, and the public good atrophy.

The Primacy of Self-Interest

The premise of singularity that shapes the core of free market schooling is a staunch belief in the primacy of self-interest. Critics of traditional public education posit the individual and advancing the needs of the individual as the rightful, only, function of schooling. Privatization and its emphasis on individual worth and wealth supports the circular reasoning that superior-quality schooling is inherent in the differences of private schools simply because these schools are private.

But the nature of these "specific differences are almost never examined; instead, readers are left to assume that private schools are somehow superior in their effectiveness" (Lubienski & Weitzel, 2008, pp. 475–476). Like other tall tales, this story falls apart when the assumptions of ideologues about the superiority of privatization cannot demonstrate superior student academic performance on weak and "noisy" standardized tests compared to results from traditional public education (Rouse & Barrow, 2008).

NINE
What Educators Don't Know about the Free Market Hurts

Low-level information processing to assert the primacy of self-interest sets the table for four oxymorons shared in this chapter. The "how" of free market theory is exposed in, and justified by, proponents via these four. The fallacies of foolishness also emerge as the inside-out logic of each oxymoron provides a glimpse into the detrimental outcomes that accompany implementation of the theory.

It's largely forgotten that in the late 1980s Albert Shanker proposed "an idea for a new kind of public school where teachers could experiment with fresh and innovative ways of reaching students" (Kahlenberg & Potter, 2014). Shanker made his proposal in the spirit of continuous improvement for traditional public education. His goal was to sustain the promises of traditional public education, which meant promoting "social mobility for working-class children and social cohesion among America's increasingly diverse populations" (Kahlenberg & Potter, 2014).

Shanker's vision (for what became known as *charter schools*) is the Dr. Jekyll of the history of teaching and learning in America. The Dr. Jekyll of Shanker's intention is an idealized means for realizing the promise of continuous improvement of professional practice in traditional public education.

Based on the ardent efforts of free market proponents, however, Mr. Hyde now pushes U.S. education toward the brink. Transformed by adherents who claim charter schools as one among many mechanisms belonging to privatization, Shanker's intention is lost.

In place of continuous improvement and service to all U.S. students in traditional public education and operationalized by mechanisms of the free market, Mr. Hyde unleashes four oxymorons embedded in free market schooling upon unsuspecting families, students, communities, and our nation's future: UnChoice, state discrimination, inefficient efficiency, and failing academic success.

UnChoice

A foundational premise of privatization is that parents have a right to choose a school that conforms to family values. This article of faith is anchored in a perception. Free market schooling adherents perceive that a right to choose schooling is created when U.S. families choose their residences based on the perceived quality of local schools (Levin, 2002).

From this practice for selecting residences, free market advocates contrive the existence of a right to choose a school unrelated to the location of the residence in which participation or enrollment can be restricted to a family's preferred racial, socioeconomic, ethnic, or religious cohort. This so-called right is the oxymoron referred to here as *UnChoice*.

UnChoice accompanies privatization in that the advertised promise of unlimited individual choice of schooling is subject to ideological, prejudicial, and/or intentional restrictions which ensure that certain individuals and families have no choice (Singer, 2017).

Although privatization proponents are loath to acknowledge any restrictions, limitations, or prohibitions on what is touted as free choice in a free market, the fact of the matter is that limits on school enrollment and school availability established by the processes and priorities of privatization ensure that UnChoice is offered to American families by the purported free market. UnChoice is unleashed by a number of factors: the nature of the U.S. housing market, the escape to bigotry, and social engineering.

The U.S. Housing Market

UnChoice is facilitated by a U.S. housing market infected with the blatant denial of rights. When free market schools locate near, or move closer to, selected neighborhoods, profit-seeking drives restricted enrollment. The tendency of the free market schools to gravitate to wealthy, White neighborhoods demonstrates willful allegiance to racist behaviors, discriminatory practices, and restrictive legislation endemic to the U.S. housing market throughout our nation's history.

Redlining, other discriminatory housing practices, and de jure or de facto segregation (Cowen et al., 2013; Loeb, Valant, & Kasman, 2011) based on race, religion, class, ethnicity, and/or income nurture UnChoice. Free market proponents abandon ethics when claiming that choices made in association with existing housing patterns (whether for schooling or housing) substantiate the claim that this is a "right" enjoyed by all in the United States. Residents of neighborhoods where poverty and/or segregation are daily facts of life cannot claim the same "right."

The Escape to Bigotry

Moreover, UnChoice facilitates the bigotry of those opposed to countervailing efforts through statute or rule to balance individual and public goods in traditional public schools. Proclaiming the right of UnChoice offers coded language to reassure those who respond to FUD, and/or who seek the segregation and denial of rights to "others" embedded in the so-called right of individual/family bias (Klein, 2017; Levin, 2002).

Marketeers claim that societal, governmental, and educational efforts to ensure the rights of all students in traditional public education—protections, mandates, and court rulings covering desegregation, special education, English Language Learning, alternative education, Title IX, LGBTQ rights, religion in public schools, and equity of school funding—are governmental overreach because the "right" already exists—UnChoice—for anyone to choose any location for their home.

The escape to bigotry stems from the refusal of individuals and families to be subject to the equity and equality established over the past several decades in traditional public education. The escape to bigotry stems also from the political and policy-making power exercised by free market advocates in statue and rule that acquiesces to bigotry and abandons democracy as the guarantor of equality.

Privatization adherents fear that statutory and regulatory requirements for equal access promoted by traditional public education colleagues, and included in statutory mandates tied to the promises of U.S. democracy, establish "increased uniformity of schools [which] reduced parental options and the ability to match child-rearing preferences of parents to school experiences" (Levin, 2002, p. 161).

At the core of this my-side bias thinking is the free market premise that the growth of social justice and equality in our traditional public schools constitutes an unjustified governmental intrusion into the right to choose schools based on any of the biases within so-called traditional family values (Levin, 2002). The free market faithful perceive that developments to safeguard equal rights in U.S. society and traditional public education over the last six decades trample another supposed right: escape to bigotry.

Social Engineering

Lurking within the outcomes of free market theory are choice schooling policies and practices redolent of social engineering.

Private schools accepting vouchers are more likely to include White students in their enrollment compared to Hispanic or African American students (Cowen, Fleming, Witte, & Wolf, 2012). The gradual, unacknowledged creep of social engineering is illuminated in data from Indiana. During the 2011–2012 school year—the first year of vouchers in the Hoosier state (camouflaged under the official title "Choice Scholarship Program")—voucher students were 46 percent White and 24 percent African American. During the sixth year of vouchers, 60 percent of voucher students were White and 12 percent were African American.

The largest voucher program of its kind in the United States, Indiana's "Choice Scholarship Program" epitomizes the social engineering developing within free market schooling. Throughout the country, students from families with elevated income levels and with parents who have attended college are more likely to attend private schools than are students from families that are actively religious (Cowen et al., 2012).

As the second decade of the twenty-first century nears its conclusion, social engineering emerges in data that shows state subsidies for enrollment in choice schools are received increasingly by families whose income allows them to pay tuition even without financial support from sources created by proponents of the free market.

State Discrimination

Proponents of the free market for education proclaim that individuals have the right not only to UnChoice but also to tax dollars to support this oxymoron and the socially engineered schools of the free market. Studies illustrate that parents choose voucher schools based on low Black enrollment even when it is not clear that these schools provide an upgrade for their children in terms of academic performance (Loeb, Valant, & Kasman, 2011, p. 153). This situation stands as a stark illustration of outcomes that attend an oxymoron that ought to be legally and morally repugnant in U.S. democracy: state-sponsored discrimination.

Statutory acquiescence to the exercise of family bias and, thus, state discrimination, is woven into the mechanisms of privatization detailed in model bills from ALEC. State discrimination is aided and abetted by statutes where language implies that all families and students have a de jure right to choose privatization. Yet, as research and data indicate, these statutes establish de facto state discrimination because tax dollars fund mechanisms that are available, in reality, only to limited cohorts of Americans.

Learners Lose When State Discrimination Occurs

Research bears out the extent to which free market mechanisms play a role in this level of discrimination. For example, several studies indicate the negative effect of student/family mobility on student achievement and the difficulty of choice schools and the ideology of the free market to deal effectively with this significant problem for learners (Cowen et al., 2012, pp. 233–234).

In Milwaukee, AfricanAmerican students are most likely to transfer out of voucher schools than any other ethnic group (Cowen et al., 2012, p. 234). In Indiana, Black student voucher participation fell from 24 percent to 14 percent in just one year (Colombo, 2015).

Black students enrolled in choice schools in Minneapolis/St. Paul during the 2010–2011 school year were twice as likely as their peers in traditional public education to attend a segregated school (Butrymowicz, 2013b). "In general, minorities and the poor are less likely to choose, unless the [voucher] plan is restricted to these groups" (Levin, 2002, p. 167).

Two fiscal factors embedded in the alleged efficiencies of the free market play a significant role in the development and maintenance of state discrimination. The first of these is that most private, often religious, schools that accept vouchers provide little or nothing in the way of transportation to and from school.

Transportation for extra-curricular participation—either immediately after school or involving travel for sports—often is not provided. Poor families initially impressed with the promises and myths of stealth-schooling find that they and their children are truly left behind when transportation is unavailable.

A second equally difficult factor is that while vouchers provide some degree of funding for private school tuition, the amount available from the state to support any individual student usually falls short of the full amount required for tuition and related costs of stealth-schooling. This minor or nonexistent issue for families at higher income levels is, for families in poverty, nothing less than state discrimination.

Furthermore, when free market mechanisms funnel more money to choice schools at the expense of traditional public education, the state discriminates against students enrolled in traditional public schools. This imbalance, from the perspective of legal scholars, denies the intent of state constitutions to provide equitable education to all children (Long, 2018).

Robust state discrimination in Michigan works with the same segregating effect. In "districts that participate in choice, white and more affluent parents have fled as poorer, minority kids have come into their schools, exacerbating de facto segregation" (Strauss, 2015). A bill passed out of the Michigan House meant "shutting down mostly traditional public schools, which in Detroit serve the neediest students, and further desert students in neighborhoods where charters have largely declined to go" (Mead, 2016).

The marketplace adherents who speak glowingly about families, and choices, and efficiency engage in nothing less than double-talk when the effect of the marketplace is to ensure that taxpayers fund the resegregation of U.S. education and social stratification that asserts White privilege.

While legislators and plutocrats may claim that this represents an unintended consequence of free market theory, these privatization proponents do little or nothing to reverse trends toward state discrimination. The losses experienced by students through state discrimination unmask free market schooling as an ethical and fiscal fraud.

When selected or preferred individuals and cohorts are paid by the state to attend private schooling, and when other individuals and cohorts in society are left out of this state funding loop, state discrimination, an oxymoron for our democracy if ever there was one, is alive and well in the United States.

Inefficient Efficiency

Free market proponents eagerly trumpet efficiency as a distinguishing feature of privatization. But, efficiency is an impression in search of reality and the oxymoron that takes hold when the free market is at work becomes *inefficient efficiency*. Independent observers and researchers cannot find efficiency in either the free market or choice schooling.

For example, studies are unable to verify that "productive efficiency is maximized when schools produce a given level and type of education for the least cost" (Belfield & Levin, 2005, p. 554). Additional research suggests that efficiency is not a readily identifiable attribute of vouchers (Barrow & Rouse, 2008; Cowen et al., 2012). Further, scholars pinpoint inefficiencies in that voucher programs are not cost neutral and can exceed the cost of the existing public school system (Rouse & Barrow, 2008).

Persistent claims by proponents that choice is the epitome of efficiency erode further when findings indicate that vouchers are the next-to-worst among twenty-two cost-effective approaches for raising student achievement (Yeh, 2010). Ranking below undeniably costly structures such as full-day kindergarten, cross-age tutoring, teacher salary, and an additional school year for all students, voucher programs rank worst in terms of cost-effectiveness with only charter schools ranking less efficient (Yeh, 2010, p. 43).

Failing Academic Success

Advocates of the free market sometimes claim that choice schooling provides superior academic results compared to traditional public schools.

However, numerous studies find that *failing academic success* is a robust oxymoron that best describes the academic results from the market. Multiple studies find no significant difference between achievement in traditional public schools and free market schools (Abdulkadiroglu et al., 2015, p. 2; Brown, 2017; DeBray-Pelot, Lubienski, & Scott, 2007; Cowen et al., 2012; Figlio & Hart, 2010; Loeb, Valant, & Kasman, 2011; Lubienski,

2013; Rouse & Barrow, 2008). A national study conducted by CREDO (Center for Research on Education Outcomes) near the end of the first decade of the twenty-first century indicated that choice schools compare negatively with traditional public schools in terms of academic proficiency (CREDO, 2009).

Four years later, CREDO's next national study of the impact of stealth-schooling—focusing on charter schools—found that charter schools did not create any learning advantage for its students compared to traditional public education (CREDO, 2013, p. 83).

The CREDO (2013) study also found that charter students who either enrolled during the year of the 2009 study, or who advanced into grades where standardized testing was required, did worse on assessments four years later even when compared to students in charters established before the 2009 CREDO study. The 2013 study also identified enduring trends for charters: "low-performing schools are not being shut quickly enough and some low-performing schools are being permitted to replicate" (CREDO, 2013, p. 83).

Data emerging near the close of the second decade of the twenty-first century suggest that stealth-schooling persistently denies students opportunities to reach high levels of academic proficiency. "In the last couple of years, a spate of studies show that voucher programs in Indiana, Louisiana, Ohio, and Washington, D.C. hurt student achievement—often causing moderate to large declines" (Barnum, 2017b).

None of this should be a surprise. Failing academic success—a disastrous oxymoron for the learning and lives of students—is of little concern to proponents of a theory designed to benefit adults. Rock-bottom achievement results in Florida, for example, do not curtail payment of scholarship monies from the state to private schools (Klein, 2017).

The presence of this oxymoron in the pantheon of privatization outcomes leaves some leaders among the free market faithful adamant that choice advocates should avoid mentioning student achievement or data-based school performance (Finn, Hentges, Petrilli, & Winkler, 2009). Never shy about playing both sides of the achievement-and-testing-fence (privatization adherents chastise traditional public education for not making the grade on standardized tests), academic results garnered in choice schools are a maybe-yes, maybe-no, point of superiority.

Using Oxymorons in the Free Market

The term *useful oxymorons* is, obviously, an oxymoron. However, free market proponents manage to turn the four oxymorons discussed earlier into paeans to the marketplace for choice education.

For example, marketeers celebrate one element of an oxymoron (e.g., "efficiency") without giving credence to the other side of the contradiction (e.g., "inefficiency"). Emphasis on the pure free market aspects of any oxymoron, moreover, gives privatization adherents plausible deniability if and when the less advantageous side of the oxymoron comes into view.

This two-sided approach also allows ideologues to take advantage of the compulsive search by society and parents/caregivers for panaceas in teaching and learning. My-side bias facilitates the extent to which this search for a schooling silver bullet can justify bigotry in the guise of ideological purity and family values.

This now-you-see-it-now-you-don't approach to oxymorons extends to additional situations created by the behaviors of free market enthusiasts. In an example from the corporate world, gas and coal subsidies from the U.S. government worth billions of dollars, and government contracts awarded for hundreds of millions of dollars, are accepted without complaint and without reference to less government by companies and businesses owned by ardent free marketeers like the Koch brothers or the Mercer family (Mayer, 2017).

Supporters of free market theory and its outcomes consider all wealth acquisition to be their just rewards. The fact that wealth accumulates for proponents in business and education through what amounts to government intrusion is not acknowledged. Oxymoronic behavior like this by free market adherents is standard operating procedure if government intrusion increases individual wealth because wealth is provided to individuals who promote less government (Mayer, 2017, p. 261).

Finally, useful oxymorons emphasize one "side" of these dichotomies while turning a blind eye to the other "side." This ensures the salience of pure concepts in pursuit of the free market. It is not a surprise that tsunamis of cash pay to highlight a false alignment with apple-pie-esque constructs like efficiency and achievement because marketeers need to camouflage Mr. Hyde, an ever-present figure in the market.

TEN
Students Sold Short in the Free Market

Knowing about the intents and outcomes of free market theory in choice education allows us to turn to a discussion of the effect of free market theory on students. As we have already seen, free market mechanisms are adult-centric manifestations of schooling devoted to the primacy of self-interest. Who can enroll in choice schools and how the free market manipulates enrollment reveal where students stand in the free market.

Segregation in the Free Market

Free market theory makes ample room for and encourages "schools that can be segregated by academic ability and disability, ethnicity, economics, language, and culture" (Underwood & Mead, 2012, p. 5). Studies illuminate "the prevalence of resegregation and the resultant inequality caused by school choice" (Dawkins-Law, 2014, p. 3).

Free market advocates camouflage segregation by claiming that school choice is family-originated and, thus, a well-established right of parents to do what's best for their children. Wrapped within this premise, however, is a less than saccharine outcome. A bitter aftertaste develops when privatization proponents extol the enrollment practices of choice schooling and "generally favor allowing participating schools to accept or deny applicants as they see fit" (Finn et al., 2009, p. 9).

Students are unwitting participants in social engineering achieved when the exclusivity of enrollment practices and a reliance on so-called family rights merge in the implementation of vouchers and other mechanisms of choice schooling across the United States. Designed more than a half-century ago as a way for White families to dodge court-ordered desegregation, vouchers financed White flight—starting in Virginia as grants to White families (Goldstein, 2015)—to religious schools with dubious academic foundations.

In the same way that vouchers were originally promulgated to provide White families with the opportunity to avoid schools where minority students are enrolled (Dawkins-Law, 2014), the intent and mechanisms of privatization sustain this outcome into the current century.

Segregation Academies Redux

Georgia's corporate tax credit program, for example, was established to benefit Latino and African American families but now awards most scholarships from this program to White well-to-do families (Fischer & Peters, 2016). Present-day outcomes like this echo the widespread appearance of "segregation academies" that developed in the South in the twenty years following *Brown v. Board of Education* (1954).

Prevalent in Mississippi, Arkansas, Alabama, and Virginia, these so-called academies were designed with the express purpose of enabling White students to avoid classroom attendance with African American students. Astonishingly, many of these continue operating to the present day as chilling testimony to the intents and outcomes of free market theory and its mechanisms (Carr, 2012).

School Practices for Social Engineering

Charter schools practice their own form of socially engineered segregation. Success Academies—often touted as New York City's most successful charters—make a practice of telling certain families that their children are not the right fit for these schools (Green, E., 2018, p. 15). To ensure a preferred configuration of the student body, Success Academies do not allow new enrollments partway through a school year in grade levels five through twelve.

This means that if a student enrolled in a Success Academy leaves after the start of the school year, the school will not "backfill" that student's enrollment place by bringing on-board students from the waiting list (Green, E., 2018). These practices "sometimes entail putting the network's organizational interests ahead of the broader well-being of students" (Green, E., 2018, p. 16).

PROFIT AND LOSS IN THE FREE MARKET

Virtual schools—a mechanism established in the free market—are promoted as models of free market efficiency. Full-time virtual schools and virtual charter schools operated by companies like K12, Inc. and Connections Academy enroll tens of thousands of students in states across the country. Online free market schools sell themselves as paragons of academic, financial, and organizational efficiency.

Again, U.S. students pay a heavy price for their free market schooling enrollment. For instance, in Pennsylvania, the state that hosts virtual charter schools in the heaviest concentration, research "found that students in charter schools were making significantly smaller gains in learning over time than matched students in traditional public schools" (Miron & Urschel, 2012, p. 5).

Children and young people enrolled in K12, Inc. schooling earn reading and math scores well below averages of students in traditional public education. Moreover, data shows that K12, Inc. students have an on-time graduation rate of 49.1 percent while traditional public education students graduate at a 79.4 percent rate in the states where K12, Inc. operates virtual schools (Miron & Urschel, 2012, p. vi).

Free Lunch, Anyone?

Costs are levied on students and families who are lured by the purported efficiencies of virtual schools spawned by free market theory. While financial and lifelong costs fall on the shoulders of students, proponents of privatization rake in fiscal profit.

Based on evidence from Ohio and other states about virtual privatization, who says there's no such thing as a free lunch? Online privatization appears to be a reincarnation of this old-fashioned come-on from tavern owners in that vendors and companies who operate virtual schools "receive the same per-pupil funding as physical schools, but operate entirely online" (Binelli, 2017, p. 17) without delivering any outcome of substance to students.

A composite picture of costs of virtual schooling—for students and for society—emerged in Ohio. The twelve thousand students throughout the Buckeye State enrolled in The Electronic Classroom of Tomorrow experienced the reality of virtual education when this online school—billed as the largest high school in America—closed in the middle of the 2017–2018 school year (Hefling, 2018a).

The State of Ohio claims that the school must pay back almost $80 million from the previous two school years because "thousands of students weren't logging on to their computers for long enough to justify what the state paid to the school" (Hefling, 2018a). An outside attorney was appointed by a judge to oversee the financial management of the school while the Ohio State Supreme Court also is involved in the matter (Hefling, 2018a).

This means, as Ohio's example indicates, that "some of the largest cyber charter companies are bringing in multi-million-dollar annual revenue streams" (Elder, 2014). This online cash cow finds K12, Inc., again, milking states and short-changing students through cost-cutting strategies such as "having more students per teacher and by reducing overall spending on teacher salaries and benefits, particularly for special instruction" (Miron & Urschel, 2012, p. iv).

Corporations eagerly belly up for the free lunch offered to their bottom line by the free market. K12, Inc. indicates that between fiscal years 2012 and 2013 company profit grew by tens of millions of dollars (Miron & Urschel, 2012).

Braggadocios in the finest traditions of the self-aggrandizing ethos of the free market, K12, Inc. claims that the efficiencies inherent in the exercise of the free market and virtual schooling ensure continued healthy profit "without any adverse effects on student performance, employee retention, customer satisfaction, or our growth rate" (Miron & Urschel, 2012, p. vii). No data exist to verify an academic profit for students enrolled in virtual schools.

The Cost of Non-Attendance

Additional studies reveal that virtual school enrollment is often a fleeting school experience. In Colorado, three times as many students drop out of online schools compared to traditional public schools. Moreover, four times as many of Colorado's online dropouts leave school permanently compared to the average for traditional public schools (Miron & Urschel, 2012).

The Legislative Auditor in Minnesota's evaluation of online schools from 2011 "found that students in full-time online schools had low course completion rates and elevated school drop-out rates" (Miron & Urschel, 2012, p. 5). For free market mavens, however, these are the statistics of profitable ignorance; collateral academic damage alongside a robust bottom line for business are commonplace.

Students Pay More Than School Fees

The costs associated with choice schooling in New Orleans are instructive when it comes to understanding implementation of free market theory instead of traditional public education. At first, test results from a new batch of charter schools in New Orleans's Recovery School District (RSD) quickly morphed into a tale about an academic miracle created by privatization in the Crescent City (Gabor, 2015).

While self-serving fables fixated on high scores on Louisiana's standardized test, charter school results were linked to questionable student enrollment tactics to boost test scores including "suspensions, pushouts, skimming, counseling out, and not handling special needs kids well" (Gabor, 2015, p. SR3). Ironically, even though exclusionary tactics and teaching-to-the-test did yield increased scores for students allowed to continue their enrollment, it turns out that Louisiana's test standards are near the bottom when compared to the rest of the nation (Gabor, 2015).

In addition, results from a national examination, the ACT, confirm the dubious academic value of improved state scores in the free market schools of New Orleans. Students in the RSD earned an average composite score of 16.4 on the ACT, "well below the minimum score required for admission to a four-year public university in Louisiana" (Gabor, 2015, p. SR3).

Amidst these costs, dropout rates could not be calculated because coherent data collection among and between the charter schools in the Recovery School District did not occur. Information about student performance in the RSD is so filled with gaps and inaccuracies that a privatization-friendly research entity, the Cowen Institute for Public Education Initiatives, "was forced to retract a study that concluded that most New Orleans schools were posting higher-than-expected graduation rates and test scores" (Gabor, 2015, p. SR3).

Social Costs Piled Upon Academic Deficits

Astonishing as it may seem, the cost of virtual schooling in the free market includes segregation. The virtual schools operated by K12, Inc. enroll far fewer free and reduced lunch students, fewer English language learners, and significantly fewer students with moderate/severe disabilities than do traditional public schools (Miron & Urschel, 2012).

"The data from K12's fully-managed schools indicates that three-quarters of the students are white" (Miron & Urschel, 2012, p. 11). The cost of low-quality academics and segregation levied on students enrolled in virtual schooling does not lead to any corresponding penalty for the companies who operate these schools. So lax is the oversight of virtual schooling that Miron and Urschel (2012) reported that "one thing we learned from our analysis is that it is not possible to explain fully how K12 Inc. spends the public resources it receives using the federal finance dataset" (p. 7).

WHERE HAVE ALL THE STUDENTS GONE? GONE TO ROI, EVERYONE!

Return on Investment (ROI) is a feature of the free market. Corporations investing in the free market for schooling expect ROI from multiple sources including tax breaks and profit. Moreover, ROI from privatization is a gift that keeps on giving because the mechanisms for enhanced profit are a work in progress thanks to ongoing statutory assistance with the potential for ever greater returns.

Corporate and Sectarian ROI from the Free Market

ROI accompanies the implementation of free market schooling regardless of the organization operating the school. Analysis reveals that "about 75 percent of voucher schools across the country are religious" (Klein, 2017, p. 4). Additional research indicates that "about half the students attending charter schools go to one that is privately corporate-managed" (Stitzlein, 2017).

This trend is replicated across the realm of choice schooling where over 80 percent of students in private schools attend a school operated by a religious organization and in some states (Indiana is one example) nearly 100 percent of voucher schools are schools with a religious affiliation (Kaufman, 2017; Smith, 2017).

In one case when a two-campus charter school in Ft. Wayne, Indiana, not only lost its charter due to dismal academic performance but also had its charter revoked, the directors of the charter simply "converted" the institution to a private, religious school. From there, the directors set about the process of securing funding from the State of Indiana in the form of private school vouchers.

ROI versus RTS

The ROI that so enthralls the free market does not tell the complete story about returns generated by choice schooling. The Return to Students (RTS) from the free market frequently falls in the debit column.

Michigan's ROI Story

An accounting of ROI affecting children and young people who participate in Michigan's choice schools, for example, serves as a grim ledger beyond dollars and into the lives and futures of students. The 2016 report from the Education Trust-Midwest found that "Michigan's K-12 system is among the weakest in the country and getting worse" (Binelli, 2017, p. 7).

It's purely Michigan schooling, where money-makes-right investments nurture a statewide educational landscape where outcomes regularly include "financial risk, including waste, fraud and abuse, lack of accountability over federal funds and lack of assurances that the schools were implementing federal programs in accordance with federal requirements" (Gorman, 2016).

This teaching and learning nightmare reveals the cost of deregulation in a free market; 80 percent of charter schools in Michigan are run by for-profit management companies. Studies of Michigan's choice schools yield "evidence that charters have actually increased inequality" (Binelli, 2017, p. 8) and fail to reduce the achievement gaps between student cohorts. These costs afflict students in charter schools throughout the state.

The disastrous cost to students emerging from Michigan's dedication to ROI affects all students. Throughout the state, "new national assessment data suggest Michigan is witnessing systemic decline across the K-12 spectrum. White, black, brown, higher-income, low-income—it doesn't matter who they are or where they live" (Binelli, 2017, p. 7).

Michigan's 2017 test scores ranked last among all fifty states in terms of student proficiency improvement. The practice of dispensing armloads of cash to support an ideology enamored of its own mechanisms yields an RTS where "70 percent of Michigan charters were in the bottom half of the state's rankings" (Binelli, 2017).

Observers who study charter schools note that free market schooling initiatives in Michigan are counterproductive. "The best-case scenario is that they don't work. And the worst-case scenario is they're actually worse than the alternatives" (Westervelt, 2016).

Federal Dollars and ROI

The U.S. Department of Education backs budget proposals that, late in the second decade of the twenty-first century, offered vouchers and charter schools an increase of $517 million while allocating another $250 million for a choice program for private schools (Hefling, 2017, p. 4).

Dollars for traditional public education in this same proposal came with a catch: traditional public school districts could access dollars from federal grants totaling $1 billion if the districts are "willing to implement 'open enrollment' programs (allowing students to attend any area public schools, charters included, and take allotted state and federal funds with them)" (Binelli, 2017, p. 8).

Analysis of the objectives associated with the federal budget suggest to observers that national leaders "seem concerned less with measuring whether schools help students learn and more with whether parents have an opportunity to pick a school for their children" (Brown, 2017). To this end, the federal budget proposed another $1 billion in new funding for grants to states called Opportunity Grants destined for private and public school choice programs (Ujifusa, 2018a).

WHAT WE CAN DO: PROCLAIM RTS AND
HOW TO THINK AS "PROFIT"!

Traditional public educators are in this current position, in part, because fiscal profit and reduced costs drive the free market. This suggests that demonstrating RTS as a profit to both individuals and society ought to be a priority. It also makes sense to share the costs associated with ROI.

- *Turnabout is fair play.* It's long past time to demand that privatization proponents own up to the shoddy academic results that constitute a significant and long-term cost of the schooling that develops from a fixation on ROI. Further, it's long past time to counter the inaccuracies of free market schooling advocates that imply the worst about traditional public education.

The time has come, therefore, for colleagues to turn the mirror of reality toward free market proponents and ask any number of questions including: How much state funding do you receive per pupil? How has this funding been spent? What specific examples are there to prove that this spending creates high quality instruction and discernible academic improvement?

What definition of thinking orients quality instruction daily at your school? Is your school run on a for-profit basis? Who designs the curriculum that is used with your students and how much does this company/individual get paid for this service? What student achievement data demonstrate that privatization leads to higher-level thinking for all students?

- *Be civil but fight fire with fire* Traditional public education colleagues are dedicated to serving so that others benefit. Students and their families know and value this approach. But, just as turnabout is fair play when it comes to defending traditional public education, it is time to fight fire with fire when it comes to dealing with the adversaries who would destroy traditional public education.

  This means that the visible and vocal statewide demonstrations by traditional public educators in several states starting in 2018 are both appropriate and necessary actions to thwart the deleterious impact of privatization. Policy-makers and privatization proponents do not "play nice in the sandbox" when it comes to legislation and funding for traditional public education. Information—a primer unto itself for legislators and policy-makers—becomes a powerful demonstration in favor of the purpose and outcomes of traditional public education.

  This demonstration must be civil but it also must be visible and vocal to add to the information and energy that parents, caregivers, school partners, and other allies can use to support traditional public education.

- *It's no time to be modest.* Traditional public schools create multiple opportunities for important successes for students each day. With this in mind, make a point to share these successes with public school opponents.

  This can be done by sending the regular communications for parents and caregivers (which should include data and information about successes in each edition) to politicians, business leaders, media outlets, and others who are vocal in their support of privatization.

Create a database of known adversaries of traditional public education to ensure that they, too, learn about the outstanding efforts and outcomes that exemplify the pursuit of *how to think*. Because traditional public education colleagues share positive facts/information on a regular basis with school communities anyway, why be modest about accomplishments and why not share data and specific examples about these positive outcomes with adversaries?

- *Spread the good news.* Many neighborhoods, homeowners' associations, villages, towns, and cities operate electronic "sites" (e.g., Facebook, *NextDoor*, various local apps, Instagram, Twitter).

  Supply these community outlets with the school information that have already created for other audiences. Excerpting what is written for parents and caregivers and sending it to community resources gives traditional public education colleagues outreach to families and citizens well beyond individual school communities.

Providing this information to senior living centers or other organizations that serve patrons who are unlikely to have students in traditional public schools allows important and positive details to reach people whose lives are improved when high-quality traditional public education is offered in the community.

TEACHER SNAPSHOT: CAROL MARSH

In my first job, assistant principal in an elementary school of a thousand students, I was quickly introduced to lunch duty and to an extraordinary "teacher/mom." Carol Marsh was a compassionate, alert, smart colleague whose dedication to our students was a lesson unto itself. I learned quickly that lunch duty allowed me to spend as much time as I could making personal contacts with students. Not only were my conversations and interactions over grilled cheese and square pieces of pizza entertaining, they gave me insights into how best to make a difference for each student.

It was Carol who provided a particularly valuable lesson regarding one of our fourth-grade students, Tom. Tom's severe scarring was apparent. He always wore long sleeves, but clearly had suffered severe burns on his arms, hands, and face. Tom seemed to self-segregate during lunch. When students would try to join him at his lunch table, Tom moved elsewhere.

I shared my concerns about Tom with Carol. I asked my veteran colleague how we could help him. She smiled and asked me to come by her classroom later in the day, after lunch.

Once I walked into Carol's class, I wasn't completely sure what to look for. Students were avidly on-task, a tribute to Carol's experience and professionalism! After just a couple of minutes, however, I began to see the pattern in Carol's classroom routine. She was constantly on the move among her charges. Every time Carol walked by Tom, she would lightly touch his hand, then his arm, patting the hand and lightly rubbing the arm. Tom began to smile every time Carol approached.

Such a simple thing but a very big reaction and interaction with Tom. The other students began to adopt her approach by shaking Tom's hand or patting him on the arm to say hello. For Tom and his classmates, lunch evolved into full tables of fourth graders without any outliers. Carol's wise and student-centered focus engaged how to think in an indirect way to the improvement of the cognition and behaviors of each and every student.

ELEVEN

Subtlety in the Free Market: "Yeah, but..."

A grade-school friend had a habit of denying the worth of anything he didn't like with a two-word phrase: "Yeah, but." If someone said her favorite subject was math and my pal hated math, the rejoinder was, "Yeah, but our teacher's a real jerk." When someone said The Dave Clark Five was the greatest rock and roll band, my friend replied, "Yeah, but they look like nerds."

The ease with which free market proponents advocate on behalf of choice schooling incorporates a facile "Yeah, but" aimed at fundamental characteristics of U.S. democracy. Concepts riveted to democracy in the United States—freedom, individual rights, free enterprise, profit—are advertised as if they are benefits of the free market.

But, the mechanisms of the free market and its advocates deliver a swift "Yeah, but" to principles fundamental to covenant and *how to think*. First, the sustained refusal of privatization advocates to countenance the worth of traditional public education is anchored in denial of the public good.

Next, denial of the worth of inalienable rights is expressed in the exclusionary, me-first ethos of privatization. Third, denial of the inclusivity galvanized to the American Dream is in play because the free market thrives when it crafts exclusionary outcomes. Finally, denial of the right of all students to cognitive agency sufficient to choose the cost of the public good, and necessary to social justice, is facilitated by fiscal shenanigans that permit the defunding of traditional public education.

Denying the Public Good

Those who assault traditional public education do so by denying the ethical and practical value of *e pluribus unum*. Denial, in this instance, is rejection of democracy's requirement for balancing individual and public goods. Only individual self-interest is of worth to privatization ideologues.

Insidiously, privatization advocates turn the tables on the nature of the public good. Free market schooling proponents reason that the public good manifest in traditional public education denies a right to connect tax-dollar funding with my-side bias laden with prejudicial beliefs. The implication, however spurious, is that traditional public education usurps an alleged right to deny social justice, liberty for all, and *e pluribus unum*.

Privatization wraps the primacy of self-interest in a mantle of exclusivity and calls it a right. The clear intention of model bills created by ALEC is to transfer "funds and control to the private sector [while they] are couched in the language of accountability, parent and family *rights*, or scholarships/vouchers" (Anderson & Donchik, 2016, p. 346).

Denial of the primary purpose of traditional public education and the meaning of its relationship with American democracy is fundamental to the private sector within the free market. Those who buy into the impressions purveyed by stealth-schooling are given license thereby to deny traditional public education for its refusal to be accountable to family biases.

As a practical matter, when free marketeers push the right-to-bias Trojan horse up against the gates of traditional public education, inside lies denial of the worth of professional certification for educators; rejection of research-based curriculum and instruction; and dismissal of data that demonstrates student academic growth (Brown, 2017; Klein, 2017). Once these and other standards of traditional public education are forsaken, denial of the public good is assured.

Denying Inalienable Rights

School choice adherents are vehement that the rights of students and families are vouchsafed only when a free market for schooling exists. From the perspective of some cohorts of American society (for example, families fearing the cessation of benefits possible only via White privilege, and/or plutocrats seeking profit or enhanced wealth from the manipulation of tax dollars) this supposedly "free" market works flawlessly.

When choice advocates deny the viability of ethical imperatives within the U.S. Constitution, various federal statutes, and/or state constitutions, the nationwide applicability of civil rights and social justice disappears from marketplace schools. Our nation's declaration of a guarantee of inalienable rights, thus, is denied. Denial in the world of stealth-schooling abounds.

- The ACLU of Southern California reported in 2016 that 20 percent of the state's more than one thousand charter schools had policies that denied enrollment to students based on poor prior achievement, immigration status, or limited skills in the English language (Long, 2018).
- Research shared in 2017 demonstrated that the preponderance of charter schools in New Jersey contributed to the segregation of the state's enrollment by enrolling at least 10 percent fewer students than public schools in terms of race, lower socioeconomic status, and limited English language skills (Long, 2018).
- Additional studies illustrate segregation and inequality patterns and trends associated with the ideology of the free market and the impact of stealth-schooling (Cowen, 2010; Cowen et al., 2012; Dawkins-Law, 2014; Lubienski, 2013).

Rooted in these findings is the design of the free market for schooling where all citizens cannot access the rights that privatization proponents demand for themselves. Denial occurs every time ideologues assert that freedom and choice are rights available for all while, at the same time, enrollment limitations, academic inadequacy, and burgeoning segregation deny inalienable rights to all but the few for whom the context of a free market is intended.

Denying the American Dream

Free market theory renders a distorted sketch of the American Dream. Democracy dilettantes like the Koch brothers, members of ALEC, and well-heeled marketeers offer their fellow citizens a painting rendered with bold brush strokes to cover up the limitations of the mechanisms of privatization.

For instance, the picture displayed by adherents of the free market fails to include the detail that students with two parents in the home are more likely to stay in voucher programs than other students (Cowen et al., 2012, p. 240). Also missing from renderings created by privatization adherents is data detailing that students with two parents in the home are "more likely to accept the offer of a voucher in the first place (Cowen, 2010) and have far less difficulty meeting the additional transportation and scheduling demands in the voucher sector (Stewart & Wolf, 2011)" (Cowen et al., 2012, p. 240).

Throughout the gallery of artistic impressions created by stealth-schooling proponents, no space is devoted to the reality that charter schools in both New Orleans and Washington, D.C., enroll smaller numbers of minority students than do traditional public schools in these cities

(Lubienski, Gulosino, and Weitzel, 2009). Absent as well in this gallery are studies of choice schools in Arizona that "show that these schools often act as vehicles for 'white flight'" (Lubienski, 2013, p. 505).

The impression that a market for schooling offers freedom to exercise rights never develops for a significant portion of U.S. families once choice schooling is established. Choice advocates turn freedom upside down when the schooling market is infused with exclusionary practices that give free rein to prejudices locked within family values.

The glorification of self-interest denies the rights of others when the ideology of privatization allows "participating schools to accept or deny applicants as they see fit" (Petrilli, Finn, Hentges, & Northern, 2009, p. 9). Because choice schools have carte blanche to "serve the students they deem best-suited to their environment" (Petrilli et al., 2009, p. 9), families who take the bait of a free marketplace can experience a switch of profound proportions.

Instead of the American Dream, the effect of choice is to resegregate U.S. education, to institute further social stratification that asserts White privilege (which is the privilege inherited by most ideologues), and to maximize relative social advantage that perpetuates the marginalization of other students and families who are not so situated within our society (Lubienski, 2013).

Freedom, for privatization proponents, means exercising a right (of their own invention) to pick and choose the schooling and the privileges to which they feel entitled while denying the inalienable rights of our democracy to those deemed ineligible.

Denying Cognitive Agency

Eliminating traditional public education as an essential resource in democracy for the public good depends upon denial of the value of cognitive agency. Denying the value of cognitive behaviors and actions tied to *how to think* expresses the belief of privatization adherents that human behavior should be nothing more than aggressive self-interest (Mayer, 2017, p. 184).

Denying cognitive agency gives ideologues the opportunity to proselytize on behalf of social Darwinism and thinking-as-rejection as the best routes to individual success in the form of self-aggrandizement and protection of personal wealth (Mayer, 2017, p. 183).

Denial of Balance through Taxation

To ensure the social and political primacy of advantaged individuals, free market adherents eschew cognitive agency and a balance of individual and public goods. Devotees up the ante for citizens who don't play the free market game and jettison the pursuit of *how to think* when they play the trump card that taxation is governmental intrusion.

Emboldened by the perspective that taxes deny the right of the individual to accrue wealth, privatization proponents eagerly play the me-first card and advocate for mechanisms that reduce or eliminate taxation. Denying that an individual's wealth should be redistributed to others through taxation to meet the need for a balance between individual and public goods is ample incentive for marketeers to destroy traditional public education with every possible cutthroat move in a game that free market proponents play for keeps.

Denial of cognitive agency is one of these moves because it constitutes denial of the right of individuals to express cognitive behaviors capable of choosing and acting upon the costs (including taxation) necessary to establish balance between individual and public goods.

Denial of cognitive agency evokes the old expression "You can't have something both ways." Marketeers demand individual choice for themselves as a key element within their agenda but deny the individual choices emerging from cognitive agency when wisdom repudiates the outcomes and contexts of the free market.

Denying cognitive agency, denying the role of *how to think*, and denying the value of balancing individual and public goods give privatization adherents sufficient rationale to deny the need to pay for comprehensive traditional public education.

When fans of the free market claim that taxes constitute theft (Mayer, 2017, p. 183), or when the claim is made that all individuals should be able to make their own way to success in society regardless of individual circumstances or experienced marginalization (Mayer, 2017), denial of cognitive agency and successful intelligence take center stage alongside mechanisms.

In part, this denial reflects the belief that no government is the best government. And, denying the need for balance achieved through taxes prevents the destruction of industry and commerce to sustain and increase the existing wealth of plutocrats (Mayer, 2017). Privileged thinking like this also depends upon the preposterous assertion that obstacles to and prejudices toward the success of individuals based on race, religion, ethnicity, socioeconomic status, disability, or "I identify as . . ." status does not occur in a free market.

The characteristics of the free market that exclude, segregate, and deny are in place to assure wealth protection for privatization proponents. Using the excuse that failure to thrive in a free market is the fault of the individual who fails, marketeers design statutes and mechanisms to ensure that only a few can be the fittest. This self-fulfilling prophecy sustains the outcomes of privatization and denies the worth of *how to think*.

This perspective stacks the deck with denial that there is value when traditional public education benefits all. Pure implementation of mechanisms that promote less government and tax reduction to sustain and enhance acquired individual wealth establishes a refuge for well-heeled free market proponents. The primary purpose of traditional public education has no value for those who deny cognitive agency because it constitutes a potentially dangerous challenge to free market restrictions that ensure that the primacy of self-interest sustains and enhances existing wealth and privilege.

Denial Is Efficient, If Nothing Else

In denial, finally, privatization proponents can claim efficiency, but little else. This understanding about efficiency smooths the way for any rationale, however ludicrous, that supports the wealth-defending, citizenship-upending, my-side bias cognition lodged within the hypotheses and mechanisms of the free market.

This version of efficiency is on display in what amounts to a shrine to privatization's impact. At the David H. Koch Hall of Human Origins in Washington, D.C., climate change is one of the topics. Within this museum "an interactive game suggested that if the climate on earth became intolerable, people might build 'underground cities' and develop 'short, compact bodies' or 'curved spines' so that 'moving around in tight spaces will be no problem'" (Mayer, 2017, p. 265).

Further examples of the self-serving ethos within free market efficiency are provided by radio hosts who shill for moneyed interests in the networks of free market proponents. These voices (who claim to be paragons of common sense) indicated to their listeners at one point that proposed government regulations to improve air and water quality would include water rationing. These regulations, warned one of these commonsense posers, are "about controlling every part of your life, even taking a shower" (Mayer, 2017, p. 267).

Denial Is Never Accountable

Denial coexists with myth and oxymoron as a strategy used early and often by ALEC. Because ALEC managed to be registered as a not-for-profit 501(C)(3) corporation, it does not share the names of its members and does not share the names of those individuals and corporations who make donations. Hiding behind their not-for-profit status, ALEC's leaders can deny their deep involvement in political maneuvering of all kinds.

Legislator-members of ALEC regularly deny the influence of ALEC or brush aside the meaning and impact of their own involvement with ALEC. Denial of the external influence of ALEC, and thus denial of input from constituents of ALEC members, creates a smokescreen that hides ALEC's "ability to disseminate its influence through diffuse and dense networks made up of individual policy entrepreneurs and large and small organizations with a common ideological agenda" (Anderson & Donchik, 2016, p. 342).

WHAT TRADITIONAL PUBLIC EDUCATORS CAN DO: MEET DENIAL WITH AFFIRMATION!

Traditional public education and its advocates can find themselves boxed in by claims of the proponents of free market schooling. Although dubious at best, these claims are made about free market schooling without regard to reams of contradictory data and without caring about multiple negative outcomes for students.

As this primer illustrates, little data exists to substantiate any of the alleged benefits of the free market for schooling. In fact, the data that does exist provides plenty of opportunities to turn around the mistakes and misdirection of free market adherents:

- *Break the privatization code.* Share information regularly about the efforts of free market proponents with the PTA or PTO. Share this information with community groups affiliated with each school or school district. Share this information with business and civic partners.

    When sharing this information, be clear about what implementation of the free market means for students. Because few parents, caregivers, or citizens have any inkling about the free market—including ALEC and its allies—or its impact, this information breaks the code that hides the agenda and the deleterious impact of the free market for schooling.

- *Ask school partners and community allies for direct help.* Once publicity is given to the free market that it deserves, ask all school allies for help. Ask school partners to communicate information and their related concerns to state legislators and other politicians.

    In addition, ask for help sharing information about this free market schooling with thought leaders in the community and state. As colleagues already know, partnerships with civic/service groups in the community—read-aloud programs, community-service projects, fund-raisers for good causes—build relationships and establish mutual benefits including positive community acclaim for the primary purpose of traditional public education.

    Asking for help from allies to communicate about the deleterious impact of free market theory, and legislative allegiance to ALEC, can open dialogue about this problem when the information is delivered by a non-educator. Once traditional public school partners and allies begin to share their concerns about privatization and its negative impact on children, a self-defense effort with considerable power is created.

Traditional public educators cannot make the mistake of kowtowing to the omniscience assumed by ALEC and privatization adherents. Information about traditional public education and its virtues dissipates the smokescreen of FUD generated by free market enthusiasts. Once the air is cleared, once educators share information to create a primer about the actual benefits of traditional public education for allies and partners, the pernicious outcomes of privatization become clear.

- *Communicate with ALEC legislators.* Although ALEC does not share its membership list publicly—it is not required to do so because of its legal status as a not-for-profit 501(C)(3) corporation—there are resources that traditional public educators should use to uncover the names of ALEC member legislators from their state.

  Some of the sites that reveal ALEC membership lists are https://alecexposed.org or www.commoncause.org/democracy-wire/who-still-funds-alec. Once the individual legislators who bring ALEC and free market schooling into your state and school are discovered, share the names with parents, caregivers, school partners, and citizens.

  Ask for help from the school community to communicate with local legislators who are ALEC members. Involve school allies in communicating with legislative friends of ALEC to share data about the negative impact of the free market on the lives and futures of children in the school, school district, and community. Alert school partners who are able and willing to talk with legislators to be factual, clear, civil, and urgent.

  All data-based sharing with members and friends of ALEC in a state's legislature must include a very specific message: legislators who align with ALEC must stop the attack on students embedded in implementation of free market theory. Using data from the school and school district, ask for specific changes in legislation that will eliminate the disadvantages visited upon students by the free market.

  Establish a feedback loop (include school colleagues, parents/caregivers, and school partners) that relays how ALEC legislators respond to communications about negative ALEC-induced effects. Replies from ALEC members should be utilized as additional sources of information about the ideology and perspectives that seek the destruction of traditional public education.

- *Put the good professional reputation of traditional public educators to work.* Surveys demonstrate each year that traditional public school colleagues—in all roles—are held in high regard locally and that the information provided by colleagues is, therefore, highly reliable. This means that *all* colleagues need to get data and information about the negative effects of privatization.

All colleagues should be encouraged to speak with neighbors, friends, relatives, as well as local service, civic, and fraternal groups about the my-side bias, negative fiscal impact, and dismal achievement fostered by state legislators and state statutes when aligned with free market theory.

The damage done by free market schooling adherents should be a topic about which all traditional public education colleagues are well versed. The extraordinary benefits of traditional public education—unity of purpose, the practice of teamwork, the virtues of democracy, and the value of students applying thought to solve important problems throughout their lives—should be shared widely in the community.

Every time these benefits are shared, positive outcomes and examples of successful intelligence, data, and details must be included. When the "talk of the town" emphasizes how traditional public education prepares students to function successfully in democratic society while contributing meaningfully to a robust economy, existing support for a primary purpose and its outcomes expands well beyond a school's "four walls."

- *Enlist the influence and action of parents and caregivers.* It's also important to realize that parents and caregivers should be enlisted to provide community and civic groups with details and data about the impact of the free market and its ALEC allies at the state and national level.

  Parents and caregivers have a significant effect when they relay information to civic groups about overall excellence in a community's traditional public education. Among many different ways that parents and caregivers can help do this is by reading short paragraphs from school newsletters or websites when they report "good news" or "updates" during meetings.

- *Share specific examples about excellence in public education.* Traditional public educators must tell parents and caregivers about specific benefits for their children that are established in learning-scapes. When specific examples are shared about how instruction makes a difference for individual students, we give parents and caregivers examples that are likely to be shared with other family members and in the community. A focus on each student's ability to think is a valuable resource that must be recognized and shared.

- *Avoid "downer descriptions."* No one is perfect. No institution is perfect. Every day is not a picnic. Although these observations are true for any individual and for any profession, if/when educators make a conversational habit of emphasizing the difficulties or unresolved problems in day-to-day work, a negative presumption about traditional public education emerges.

Free market schooling proponents are only too happy to exploit every negative about traditional public education even though the daily dilemmas described are either temporary or solvable. Avoiding *any* negative habit is a wise choice; consciously asserting the important positives about the practice of traditional public education puts everyone in traditional public education in a better position to sustain the pursuit of a primary purpose while at the same time short-circuiting the negative influence of the ideology of privatization.

- *Stop FUD in its tracks.* Talk with parents, caregivers, community members, and family members to dispel fear, uncertainty, and doubt about traditional public education. Constructive and positive examples of safety, respect, and the rock-solid achievement created daily in traditional public education should be at the foundation of regular conversations.

Moreover, dealing directly with the numerous ways that traditional public education creates a safe learning environment is just one way to preempt FUD. Public education colleagues must share examples of excellence frequently because the foolishness and inaccuracy of the attack on traditional public education means this is no time to be modest.

Traditional public education colleagues must also be ready with information and data-based communications if/when a problem or a significant incident arises. Educators must be devoted to sharing with the community no matter what the perception may seem about the dilemma. Up-front communication with the school community is the best way to dispel fear, uncertainty, and doubt.

Up-front communications with the school community means that educators are not bragging about the successes of our students, the professional practices that access the capabilities and heritage of all students, or the active measures that keep students and staff secure during each school day. Sharing our successes establishes an essential counternarrative to FUD.

TWELVE

The Free Market Is a Desperate Place—Traditional Public Education to the Rescue!

The function of traditional public educators encompasses the strategies, concepts, research, data, and professional behaviors necessary to empower students with *how to think*, successful citizenship, and a substantive future. The goal of this chapter is to discuss how traditional public education rescues U.S. democracy from the bleak future visited upon U.S. students and future citizens by free market theory.

The perspective in this chapter depends on knowledge and concepts shared in the earlier segments of this primer. Traditional public education is necessary for the well-being of U.S. democracy but traditional public education is being pushed away from this role. Free market theory and its proponents deliver appealing promises but little in the way of quality education. Traditional public education and its allies must push back in the name of purpose, quality, and democracy.

PUSH BACK: PRINCIPLES FOR APPLYING THIS PRIMER

Although the free market claims mechanisms, efficiency, less government, and lower cost as its worthy attributes, the data shared throughout this discussion illustrates that free market schooling attributes have no significant impact on student learning. The context claimed by free market enthusiasts is adult-centric; students pay long-range costs while marketeers reap profit.

Understanding that the free market and its mechanisms appeal to the primacy of self-interest, and understanding that the mechanisms of the free market constitute a sinkhole instead of educational purpose, this primer provides information that give traditional public educators principles with which to launch a push back.

First Principle: RTS Is the Ultimate Added Value

When push comes to shove, what matters most to traditional public educators, and to parents/caregivers, is the Return to Students (RTS) provided by quality teaching and learning.

The data shared throughout this primer—about traditional public education and about free market schooling—presents the profound differences between ROI and RTS. Persistent, honest, straightforward information highlights the superior value of RTS compared to the self-serving ROI ballyhooed by privatization proponents.

Second Principle: Inspiring Mozarts and Einsteins and Protecting Their Noses

All colleagues in traditional public education know, because they welcome and teach all students, that *how to think* empowers the assets, capacities, and cognitive behaviors of all students as their successful intelligence is expressed throughout their lives.

Responsive cognition and cognitive agency *lead out* to the genius of democracy: all benefit when the right of an individual to swing his/her arm ends where others' noses begin. This exchange—the cost of restricted arm-swinging exchanged for unbroken noses all around—symbolizes the wealth embedded in fully realized liberty and justice for all and the values added in democracy by the universality of successful intelligence for successful citizenship.

The primacy of self-interest and my-side bias of free market schooling, by comparison, trap student cognition and exclude students with restrictions, segregation, and denial. The free market is more than the American Dream deferred, it is the American Dream abandoned.

Third Principle: Establish Function and Social Justice

The practice of traditional public education evolves. Continuous maturation of function is continuous improvement within the journey of teaching and learning toward *how to think*.

The ability to organize and prioritize cognitive behaviors that align with the most effective possible responses to student learning is the responsibility of traditional public educators and stands in sharp contrast to the stasis at the core of mechanisms at the core of free market schooling. Engaging all students with successful intelligence establishes the foundation for social justice as ideal behavior.

THIRTEEN
What It Takes to Climb Off the Limb

Dear Fellow Educators:

Any long-time educator in the PreK–12 arena has received countless "Dear Colleague" letters from the U.S. Department of Education about topics both large and small. This final chapter in this primer is in no way meant to duplicate the very formal, sometimes condescending, always complicating-our-tasks messages wrapped up in those USDOE communications.

Rather, this chapter is a letter to conclude this primer by first sharing the deep appreciation of all three authors for the colleagues with whom they've worked side by side, for the colleagues they never worked with directly but know from pursuit of a shared primary purpose, and for the women and men who will devote their lives to reaching and teaching the future represented in the lives of countless millions of U.S. children who will attend traditional public education in the decades to come.

This enduring respect for the professionalism of colleagues in traditional public education lies at the center of this primer. The efforts of traditional public educators on behalf of children and young people foster the positive possibilities in the future of each student. The well-being of students, the improvement of student thinking, the enrichment of student lives, the advancement of social justice in U.S. democracy—all arise from the professionalism of traditional public educators whose service is the finest example of enlightened self-interest.

Day-in-and-day-out traditional public educators serve to facilitate the fulfillment of U.S. democracy in a balance between individual and public goods. Nearly 90 percent of our nation's children and young people learn and improve their lives in traditional public education classrooms. Everything that happens, every decision that is made, every daily interaction directly or indirectly invokes the profession's primary purpose: *how to think*.

The worth of our cognitive behaviors as colleagues lies in positive engagement of students in learning. Traditional public education exists for students and their well-being.

The objective in this primer has been to share ideas, concepts, theories, data, and strategies that colleagues may apply as they engage in their transformative work in response to free market schooling and its proponents. The purpose of this primer was to gather information and reveal the power of this data so that traditional public educators can put these to work to thwart the teaching and learning shortfalls embedded in free market schooling. But this primer has barely touched the surface of the professional behaviors and information at the core of traditional public education that form the baseline from which to contend against free market theory.

A student-centric ethos underlies the purpose and professional practices that pursue this purpose in comprehensive traditional public education. From preventing cyberbullying to safely dealing with bodily fluid spills, from ensuring that students are vaccinated to providing nutritious meals, from fulfilling a variety of instructional mandates from state legislatures to carrying out active-shooter drills, and from instilling respect for the nation and its traditions to raising funding for programs that cannot be accommodated because traditional funding sources dry up, traditional public school professionals carry out societal imperatives that no other agency, institution, or entity can or will.

Traditional public education may be sold short by advocates of free market schooling, but the service and impact of traditional public educators are dedicated to something greater than themselves and to something more essential to democracy than blatant self-interest. Professional practice engages students with the cognitive behaviors necessary and sufficient for social justice and these engage students with habits of mind for responsive cognition and cognitive agency. Successful intelligence is the right of every student and this is a right that must take precedence across the realm of traditional public education.

Critics—policy-makers, politicians, and plutocrats invested heavily in the self-aggrandizing intentions of privatization—will take to social media to lambast the ideas shared in this primer while they continue to denigrate the value of traditional public education. This primer is, after all, a data-driven and evidence-rich condemnation of the free market and the effects of this ideology on students and American society.

This primer also reveals that free market schooling cannot escape market failure; within the nature and precepts of the free market lie its devastating and counterproductive outcomes, myths, and oxymorons.

The free market, mechanisms, reform, competition, choice—all exist to establish stealth-schooling where positive student outcomes are subservient to the intentions, demands, and self-interest of adult-centric theory. With little of academic or student-centered substance to offer, those who advocate for the end of traditional public education in the name of free market priorities will revert to name-calling and denial in response to this primer and an investment in what's best for students and their futures.

Ongoing information sharing is emblematic of the focus on what's best for students riveted to traditional public education. Improving, sustaining, and sharing professional practices required in traditional public education allows traditional public educators to substantiate the fundamental differences between the two perspectives about teaching and learning in the United States.

An intentional, classroom-by-classroom, and nationwide response to free market schooling proponents is and will be effective because it undercuts the intentions, purpose, and strategies of the adult-centric theory that infests privatization. The weaknesses of the free market (from which ideologues mount the attack on traditional public education) cannot withstand the persistent continuous improvement, the professional practice oriented by a GPPS, and the mosaic of cognitive behaviors that engages traditional public education students with the cognitive behaviors of wisdom.

The quality, purpose, and outcomes of traditional public education do need support above and beyond day-to-day professionalism. Among the most detrimental effects of the attack on traditional public education is the demoralization of teachers.

It is an oxymoron in and of itself to believe that exceptionally bright, highly qualified college and university graduates will become teachers and leaders in traditional public education in the numbers required throughout America when compensation for all roles in U.S. education is woeful and when calumny, public insult, and disdain ride in the sidecar beside the engine of inadequate pay.

The information shared throughout this primer can defend against those who assail public education when it's used to emphasize the imperative to provide adequate fiscal compensation and support for traditional public education. Data illustrates how the free market seeks the lowest common denominator for students and in schooling. When it comes to the low-bar objectives sought by free market schooling advocates, disincentivizing quality in traditional public education by reducing educator's pay is a theory-based strategy.

Ever-changing, mostly lower-order, academic targets reveal another means by which free market theory disincentivizes quality throughout America's schools. Colleagues become reluctant to seek employment in challenging school environments where the imposition of free market agenda mandates stipulate drill-and-kill instruction alongside the perception that students have little chance of academic growth or success.

Equally discouraging are the deliberately disdainful comments directed at traditional public educators by politicians, policy-makers, plutocrats, and ideological social media trolls as they force-feed the United States with free market theory.

Public support and positive regard for traditional public educators are necessary and warranted. As information explored in this primer demonstrates and as colleagues already know, support for traditional public education exists at the local level and should be tapped nationwide.

All who serve in traditional public education and across U.S. democracy have an ongoing responsibility for sustaining and enhancing this support for a primary purpose and quality professional practice in traditional public education. Ultimately, support for and understanding of the essential role of traditional public education in the future of young people and U.S. democracy abides within advancing the quality of professional practice.

Research and data speak to the positive impact of function and to the meaning of this focus in traditional public education. As a result, traditional public education colleagues cannot allow the dysfunctional reliance on the agenda of the free market to constitute a reliable and meaningful substitute for education for *how to think*. The free market agenda has nothing to do with *how to think* and even less to do with the engagement of students' cognitive behaviors in successful intelligence.

Free market theory lies at the foundation of America's counterproductive dependence on mechanisms and standardized testing. Mechanisms and standardized testing are associated outcomes of the assault on traditional public education.

Trapped by standardized testing, overwhelmed by related rules/regulations, denied mandates that facilitate *how to think*, traditional public educators are forced to fend off a detrimental and derogatory assault.

How to turn this tide? Share professional stories that embrace the student-centric data from this primer and the outcomes from day-to-day quality instruction! Speak persistently about traditional public educators who work miracles in their classrooms every day. Traditional public educators must stem the tide of negative perceptions generated by assailants by extolling the professional acumen of colleagues that fosters student success:

- children who learn to read against all odds;
- students who demonstrate complex thinking across the comprehensive subject area disciplines of STEAM (science, technology, engineering, arts, and math);
- students whose abilities to create, while collaborating, make improvement in a neighborhood possible;

- young people whose respect for a transformative adult at school is expressed in current achievements and future goals that otherwise would be illusory.

The discussion throughout this primer illustrates that traditional public educators hold the keys to curtailing the deleterious impact of free market theory: function, quality instruction, and vibrant outcomes (based on *how to think*) evidenced in the lives of students.

At the end of a long and fulfilling day in traditional public education, each traditional public educator can look back on student-centric successes and know that these examples defend students and their learning. Broadcasting a primary purpose and the professional practices that engage all students in pursuit of this purpose, educators can supplant the push from free market schooling adherents and the self-serving purposes that give rise to the implementation of stealth-schooling.

As it turns out, the core of traditional public education puts free market schooling, its purpose, and its ideology out on a limb on a very tall tree. Taking charge of the data and outcomes that represent the pursuit of *how to think*, traditional public education colleagues can sustain and grow their service to America's students. Quality professional practice provides the tools that traditional public educators require to make a difference in the thinking and the lives of all of America's students. Moreover, and with a multitude of tools at the ready, it's time to take saw in hand to make sure that the free market, privatization, and stealth-schooling take the fall they so richly deserve.

References

AASA. (2017, November 2). AASA Executive Director Responds to GOP Tax Plan. *Press Release*. Alexandria, VA: AASA. Retrieved from http://www.aasa.org/content.aspx?id-41771

AP (Associated Press). (2018, May 16). Ball State Takeover of Muncie Schools Gets $2.9M in Aid. *US News and World Report*. Retrieved from https://www.usnews.com/states/indiana/ball-state-trustees-sign-off-on-muncie-schools

Abdulkadiroglu, A., Pathak, P. A., & Walters, C. R. (2015, December). School Vouchers and Student Achievement: Evidence from the Louisiana Scholarship Program. *Working Paper 21839*. Cambridge, MA: National Bureau of Economic Research. Retrieved from http://www.nber.org/papers/w21839

Anderson, G. L., & Donchik, L. M. (2016). Privatizing Schooling and Policy Making: The American Legislative Exchange Council and New Political and Discursive Strategies of Education Governance. *Educational Policy, (30)*2, 322–364. doi:10.1177/0895904814528794

Astley, G. W. (1985). Administrative Science as Socially Constructed Truth. *Administrative Science Quarterly, 30*, 497–513. Retrieved from https://www.jstor.org/stable/pdf/2392694

Barnum, M. (2017a, June 26). First study of Indiana's voucher program—the country's largest—finds it hurts kids' math skills at first, but not over time. *ChalkBeat*. Retrieved from http://www.chalkbeat.org/posts/us/2017/06/26/first-study-of-indiana's-voucher-program

Barnum, M. (2017b, July 12). Do school vouchers "work"? As the debate heats up, here's what research really says. *ChalkBeat*. Retrieved from http://www.chalkbeat.org/posts/us/2017/07/12/do-school-vouchers-work-as-the-debate-heats-up-heres-what-research-really-says

Barrow, L., & Rouse, C. E. (2008). School Vouchers: Recent Findings and Unanswered Questions. *Economic Perspectives (3Q)*. Chicago: Federal Reserve Bank of Chicago. Retrieved from http://ssrn.com/abstract=1268316

Belfield, C., & Levin, H. (2005). Vouchers and Public Policy: When Ideology Trumps Evidence. *American Journal of Education, (111)*4, 548–567. doi:10.1086/431183

Berliner, D. C., & Biddle, B. J. (1995). *The Manufactured Crisis: Myths, Fraud, and the Attack on America's Public Schools*. New York: Addison-Wesley.

Berry, B., Johnson, D., & Mongomery, D. (2005). The Power of Teacher Leadership. *Educational Leadership, (62)*5, 56–60. Retrieved from https://eric.ed.gov/?id=EJ725886

Binelli, Mark. (2017, September 15). Michigan Gambled on Charter Schools. Its Children Lost. *The New York Times*. Retrieved from https://nyti.ms/2xLofbr

Bloom, B. (Ed.) (1956). *Taxonomy of Educational Objectives: The Classification of Educational Goals*. New York: Longmans Green.

Boesenberg, E. (2003). Privatizing Public Schools: Education in the Marketplace. *Workplace, 10*, 66–76. Retrieved from https://www.researchgate.net/315613921_Privatizing_Public_Schools_Education_in_the_Marketplace

Bolsen, T. (2013). A Light Bulb Goes On: Norms, Rhetoric, and Actions for the Public Good. *Political Behavior, 35*, 1–20. doi:10.1007/s11109-011-9186-5

Boyland, L., & Ellis, J. (2015). The Reasons That Indiana Superintendents Retire: Rhetoric and Reality. *The AASA Journal of Scholarship and Practice. (11)*4, Winter 2015. 21–38.

Bracey, G. W. (2004). *Setting the Record Straight: Responses to Misconceptions About Public Education in the United States.* Portsmouth, NH: Heinemann.

Bracey, G. W. (2009). *Educational Hell: Rhetoric vs. Reality.* Alexandria, VA: Educational Research Service.

Brooks, D. (2017, November 16). Our Elites Still Don't Get It. *The New York Times.* Retrieved from https://nyti.ms/2jz2uZD

Brown, E. (2017, April 9). DeVos Praises This Voucher-like Program. Here's What It Means for School Reform. *The Washington Post.* Retrieved from https://www.washingtonpost.com/local/education/devos-praises-this-voucher-like-program

Brown, E., & McLaren, M. (2016, December 26). How Indiana's School Voucher Program Soared, and What It Says about Education in the Trump Era. *The Washington Post.* Retrieved from https://www.washingtonpost.com/local/education/how-indianas-schools

Brown, P. C., Roediger III, H. L., & McDaniel, M. A. (2014). *Make It Stick.* Cambridge, MA: The Belknap Press at Harvard University.

Brown v. Board, 347 U.S. 483 (1954).

Burbank, M. J., & Levin, D. (2015). Community Attachment and Voting for School Vouchers. *Social Science Quarterly, (96)*5, 1169–1177. doi:1111/ssqu.12225

Butrymowicz, S. (2013a, August 22). Even in Birthplace of Charter Schools, the Grand Experiment Is at Risk. *Time Magazine.* Retrieved from www.nation.time.com/2013/08/22/even-in-birthplace-of-charter-schools-the-grand-experiment-is-at-risk

Butrymowicz, S. (2013b, July 15). A New Round of Segregation Plays Out in Charter Schools. *The Hechinger Report.* Retrieved from www.hechingerreport.org/as-charter-schools-come-of-age-measuring-their-success-is-tricky

Calsamiglia, C., Haeringer, G., & Kiljn, F. (2010). Constrained School Choice: An Experimental Study. *The American Economic Review, (100)*4, 1860–1874. Retrieved from www.iae.csic.es/investigatorsMaterial/a11222125118archivoPdf18241

Carey, K. (2017, March 2). DeVos and Tax Credit Vouchers: Arizona Shows What Can Go Wrong. *The New York Times.* Retrieved from https://www.nytimes.com/2017/03/02/upshot/arizona-shows-what-can-go-wrong-with-tax-credit-vouchers.html

Carey, K., & Harris, E. A. (2016, December 12). It Turns Out Spending More Probably Does Improve Education. *The New York Times.* Retrieved from http://nyti.ms2hfv3YM

Carr, S. (2012, December). In Southern Towns, "Segregation Academies" Are Still Going Strong. *The Atlantic.* Retrieved from https://www.theatlantic.com/national/archive/2012/12/in-southern-towns-segregation-academies-are-still-going-strong/266207

Chubb, J. E., & Moe, T. M. (1990). *Politics, Markets, and America's Schools.* Washington, DC: The Brookings Institution.

Colombo, H. (2015, February 24). Big Jump in Voucher Use for Students Who Never Tried Public School. *ChalkBeat.* Retrieved from http://in.chalkbeat.org/2015/02/24/big-jump-in-voucher-use-for-students-who-never-tried-public-school

Constitution of the United States. (nd). Retrieved from https://constitutioncenter.org

Cook, T., & Turner, K. (2015, June 7). Surprise Charter School Loan Program Raises New Questions. *The Indianapolis Star.* Retrieved from https://www.indystar.com/story/news/politics/2015/06/07/surprise/28493699

Cowen, J. M. (2010). Who Chooses, Who Refuses? Learning More from Students Who Decline Private School Vouchers. *American Journal of Education, (117)*1, 1–24.

Cowen, J. M., Fleming, D. J., Witte, J. F., & Wolf, P. J. (2012). Going Public: Who Leaves a Large, Longstanding, and Widely Available Urban Voucher Program. *American Educational Research Journal, (49)*2, 231–256. doi:10.3102/0002831211424313

Cowen, J. M., Fleming, D. J., Witte, J. F., Wolf, P. J., & Kisida, B. (2013). School Vouchers and Student Attainment: Evidence from a State-Mandated Study of Milwaukee's Parental Choice Program. *The Policy Studies Journal, (41)*1, 147–168. doi:10.1111/psj.12006

CREDO (Center for Research on Education Outcomes). (2009). *Multiple Choice: Charter School Performance in 16 States.* Stanford, CA: Stanford University.
CREDO. (2013). *National Charter School Study 2013.* Stanford, CA: Stanford University. Retrieved from http://credo.stanford.edu/documents/NCSS%202013%20Final%20Draft.pdf
Dawkins-Law, S. E. (2014). Why American Needs a Counterstory to "Choice as the Last Civil Right." *Sanford Journal of Public Policy, (5)*2, 1–20. Retrieved from https://sites.duke.edu/sjpp/files/2014/05/Dawkins-Law
DeBray-Pelot, E. H., Lubienski, Christopher A., & Scott, J. T. (2007). The Institutional Landscape of Interest Group Politics and School Choice. *Peabody Journal of Education, (82)*2–3, 204–230. Retrieved from https://gspp.berkeley.edu/assets/uploads/research/pdf/The_Institutional_Landscape_of_Interest_Group_Politics_and_School_Choice.pdf
Dewey, J. (1916). *Democracy and Education.* Retrieved from www.public-library.uk
Donheiser, J. (2017, July 18). What's ALEC? Ahead of Betsy DeVos's Speech, Here's Which States Earn the Group's Education Policy Praise. *ChalkBeat.* Retrieved from http://www.chalkbeat.org/posts/us/2017/07/18/whats-alec-ahead
Dunbar, F. (2018). Teaching Mosaic: Putting Together the Pieces of Interdisciplinary Instruction. 2018. Retrieved from https://www.amle.org/A-Teaching-Mosaic-Putting-Together-the-Pieces-of-Interdisciplinary-Instruction
Education Commission of the States. (2018). Retrieved from www.esc.org
Elder, A. (2014, January–March). Do Cyber Charter Schools Help or Hurt the Educational System? *Penn State University Education News.* Retrieved from https://www.ed.psu.edu/educ/news/january-march-2014/cyber-charter
English, L. M., & Irving, C. J. (2012). Women and Transformative Learning. In Edward W. Taylor, Patricia Cranton, and Associates (Eds.) *The Handbook of Transformative Learning: Theory, Research, and Practice,* 245–254.
Figlio, D., & Hart, C. (2010). Competitive Effects of Means-Tested School Vouchers. *Working Paper 16056.* Cambridge, MA: National Bureau of Economic Research. Retrieved from http://www/nber.org/papers/w16056
Finn, Jr., C. E., Hentges, C., Petrilli, M. J., & Winkler, A. (2009). *When Private Schools Take Public Dollars: What's the Place of Accountability in School Voucher Programs?* Washington, DC: Thomas B. Fordham Institute.
Fischer, B., & Peters, Z. (2016, March 8). ALEC Continued to Cash in on Kids in 2015 and Beyond. *PRWatch.* Retrieved from http://www.prwatch.org/news/2016/03/cashing-kids-172-alec-education-bills-2015
Fisher, D., & Frey, N. (2008). *Better Learning Through Structured Teaching: A Framework for the Gradual Release of Responsibility.* Alexandria, VA: ASCD.
Fleming, D. J., Cowen, J. M., Witte, J. F., & Wolf, P. J. (2013). Similar Students, Different Choices: Who Uses a School Voucher in an Otherwise Similar Population of Students? *Education and Urban Society, (47)*7, 1–28. doi:10.1177/0013124513511268
Foner, E. (1990). *A Short History of Reconstruction.* New York: HarperCollins Publishers Inc.
Fox, E., & Alexander, P. A. (2011). Learning to Read. In Richard E. Mayer & Patricia A. Alexander (Eds.) *Handbook of Research on Learning and Instruction,* 7–31. New York: Routledge.
Frost, R. (1942). *Collected Poems of Robert Frost.* Garden City, NY: Halcyon House.
Gabor, A. (2015, August 23). The Myth of the New Orleans School Makeover. *The New York Times.* p. 3SR. Retrieved from https://www.nytimes.com/2015/08/the-myth-of-the-new-orleans-school-makeover
Goldstein, D. (2015). *The Teacher Wars: A History of America's Most Embattled Profession.* New York: Anchor Books.
Goldstein, D. (2017, April 11). Special Ed School Vouchers May Come With Hidden Costs. *The New York Times.* Retrieved from https://myti.ms/2onz9kO

Gorman, N. (2016, December 6). Betsy DeVos: 9 Facts that Sum Up Everything You Need to Know. *Education World*. Retrieved from www.educationworld.com/a_news/betsy-devos-9-facts-sum-everything-you-need-know-1764143159

Green, E. (2018, January/February). The Charter-School Crusader. *The Atlantic*. Retrieved from https://www.theatlantic.com/magazine/archive/2018/01/success-academy-charter-schools-eva-moskowitz/546554/

Green, E. L. (2017, April 28). Vouchers Found to Lower Test Scores in Washington Schools. *The New York Times*. Retrieved from https://nyti.ms/2pemnp7

Hefling, K. (2017, October 30). How the Kochs are Trying to Shake Up Public Schools, One State at a Time. *Politico*. Retrieved from https://www.politico.com/story/2017/10/30/kochs-public-schools-shakeup-244259?cmpid=sf

Hefling, K. (2018a, January 26). States Embrace New Career and Technical Education Policies; Ohio's Virtual School Quandary. *POLITICO'S Morning Education*. Retrieved from https://www.politico.com/morning-education/2018/01/26/states-embrace-new-career-and-technical-education-policies

Hefling, K. (2018b, April 8). Oklahoma Walkout Enters Second Week/Military Groups Push Back against Voucher-like Bill. *POLITICO. Morning Education*. Retrieved from https://www.politico.com/newsletters/morning-education/2018/04/09/oklahoma-walkout-enters-second-week-162751

Herron, A., & Fittes, E. K. (2017, November 26). Why More Schools in Danger of Going Broke. *The Indianapolis Star*. pp. 1A, 6A–8A.

Hess, F. M. (2010). Does School Choice "Work"? *National Affairs*, Fall, 35–53. Retrieved from www.nationalaffairs.com/publications/detail/does-school-choice-work

Holyoak, K. J., & Morrison, R. G. (2005). Thinking and Reasoning: A Reader's Guide. In Keith J. Holyoak and Robert G. Morrison (Eds.) *The Cambridge Handbook of Thinking and Reasoning*, 1–13. New York: Cambridge University Press.

Hostetler, K. (2003). The Common Good and Public Education. Book review. In *Educational Theory, (53)*3, 347–361. doi.10.1111/j.1741-5446.2003.00347

Hunter, M. (1982). *Mastery Teaching*. Thousand Oaks, CA: Corwin Press.

Ignelzi, M. (2000). Meaning-Making in the Learning and Teaching Process. *New Directions for Teaching and Learning, 82*, 5–14. Retrieved from https://doi.org/10.1002/tl.8201

Indiana Constitution. (1851). *Constitution of the State of Indiana Article 8, Section 1*. As amended 2016. Retrieved from www.law.indiana.edu and www.iga.in.gov

Jesse, D. (2014, July 7). Michigan School Chief Promises to Get Tough with Charter School Authorizers. *Detroit Free Press*. Retrieved from http://www.freep.com/article/2014/0707/NEWS06/307070138/charter-schools-michigan-authorizers-flanagan

Jones, B. D., Thomas III, H. F., & Wolfe, M. (2014). Policy Bubbles. *Policy Studies Journal, (42)*1, 146–171. Retrieved from https://doi.org/10.1111/psj.12046

Kahlenberg, R. D., & Potter, H. (2014, August 30). The Original Charter School Vision. *The New York Times*. Retrieved from https://www.nytimes.com/albert-shanker-the-original-charter-school-visionary.html

Kaufman, B. C. (2017, February 13). School Vouchers Bring More Money to Catholic Schools—but at a Cost, Study Finds. *Notre Dame News*. Retrieved from http://news.nd.edu/news/school-vouchers-bring-more-money-to-catholic-schools-but-at-a-cost-study-finds

Kegan, R. (1980). Making Meaning: The Constructive-Developmental Approach to Persons and Practice. *The Personnel and Guidance Journal*, 373–380. doi:10.1002/j.2164-4918.1980.tb00416

Klein, R. (2017, December 26). Voucher Schools Championed by Betsy DeVos Can Teach Whatever They Want. Turns Out They Teach Lies. *HuffPost*. Retrieved from https://www.huffingtonpost.com/entry/school-voucher-evangelical

Kohlberg, L., & Hersh, R. H. (1977). Moral Development: A Review of the Theory. *Theory into Practice, (16)*2, 53–59. Retrieved from http://links.jstor.org/sici?sici=0040-5841%28197704%2916%3A2%3C53%3AMDAROT%3E2.0.CO%3B2-%23

Kolb, A. Y., & Kolb, D. A. (2009). Experiential Learning Theory: A Dynamic, Holistic Approach to Management Learning, Education, and Development. In Steven J. Armstrong & Cynthia V. Fukami (Eds.). *The SAGE Handbook of Management, Learning, Education, and Development*, 42–68. Retrieved from http://dx.doi.org/10.4135/9780857021038.n3

Krathwohl, D. R. (2002). A Revision of Bloom's Taxonomy: An Overview. *Theory Into Practice, (41)*4, 212–218. Retrieved from https://www.depauw.edu/files/resources/krathwohl

Larson, R., and Angus, R. M. (2011). Adolescents' Development of Skills for Agency in Youth Programs: Learning to Think Strategically. *Child Development, (82)*1, 277–294. Retrieved from www.youthdev.illinois.edu

Leo, U., & Wickenberg, P. (2013). Professional Norms in School Leadership: Change Efforts in Implementation of Education for Sustainable Development. *Journal of Educational Change*, 14, 403–422. doi:10.1007/s10833-013-9207-8

Leonor, M. (2018, March 22). Spending Bill Would Give Big Boost to Education. *POLITICO Morning Education*. Retrieved from https://www.politico.com/newletters/morning-education/2018/03/23/spending-bill-would-give-big-boost-to-education-147287

Levin, H. M. (2002). A Comprehensive Framework for Evaluating Educational Vouchers. *Educational Evaluation and Policy Analysis, (24)*3, 159–174. Retrieved from https://www.jstor.org/stable/3594163

Lithwick, D. (2018, February 28). They Were Trained for This Moment. *Slate*. Retrieved from https://slate.com/news-and-politics/2018/02/the-student-activists-of-stoneman-douglas-high-demonstrate-the-power-of-a-full-education

Loeb, S., Valant, J., & Kasman, M. (2011). Increasing Choice in the Market for Schools: Recent Reforms and their Effects on Student Achievement. *National Tax Journal, (64)*1, 141–164. Retrieved from https://cepa.stanford.edu/sides/default/files/A06-Loeb.pdf

Long, K. (2018). Indiana's Charter Schools: Taking a Holistic Approach to Determine Their Constitutional Legality. *Indiana Law Review, (51)*3. 797–822.

Lubienski, C. (2013). Privatising Form or Function? Equity, Outcomes and Influence in American Charter Schools. *Oxford Review of Education, (39)*4, 498–513. http://dx.doi.org/10.1080/03054985.2013.821853

Lubienski, C., Gulosino, C., & Weitzel, P. (2009). School Choice and Competitive Incentives: Mapping the Distribution of Educational Opportunities across Local Education Markets. *American Journal of Education*, 115, 601–647. Retrieved from http://www.jstor.org/stable/10.1086/599778

Lubienski, C., & Weitzel, P. (2008). The Effects of Vouchers and Private Schools in Improving Academic Achievement: A Critique of Advocacy Research. *Brigham Young University Law Review*. March 1, 2008. 2008:447–485. Retrieved from https://www.researchgate.net/263045350

Mann, H. (1839). *Report for 1839.* Annual Reports of the Secretary of the Board of Education. Retrieved from https://archive.org/details/annualreportsse00manngoog

Marzano, R. J. (2007). *The Art and Science of Teaching.* Alexandria, VA: ASCD.

Mayer, J. (2017). *Dark Money: The Hidden History of the Billionaires Behind the Rise of the Radical Right.* New York: Anchor Books.

Mayflower Compact. (nd). Retrieved from www.pilgrimhallmuseum.org

McKinney, J., & Shaffer, M. (2018, February). *Special Education in Indiana's Voucher Schools: What Are Parents Giving Up to Gain Choice?* Paper presented at the meeting of the Eastern Educational Research Association, Clearwater Beach, FL.

Mead, R. (2016, December 14). Betsy DeVos and the Plan to Break Public Schools. *Daily Comment, The New Yorker*. Retrieved from www.newyorker.com/news/daily-comment/betsy-devos-and-the-plan-to-break-public-schools

Mezirow, J. (1997). Transformative Learning: Theory to Practice. *New Directions for Adult and Continuing Education, (74)*5, 5–12. doi:10.1002/ace.7401

Mezirow, J. (2000). Learning to Think Like an Adult: Core Concepts of Transformation Theory. In Jack Mezirow, et al. (Eds.) *Learning as Transformation. Critical Perspectives on a Theory in Progress.* 3–33. San Francisco: Jossey-Bass. doi:10.1.1.463.1039

Miron, G., & Urschel, J. L. (2012, July). Understanding and Improving Full-time Virtual Schools. *National Education Policy Center, Evaluation, Planning, and Policy Analysis and Western Michigan University.* Retrieved from http://nepc.colorado.edu/publication/understanding-improving-virtual

Molden, D. C. & Higgins, E. T. (2013). Motivated Thinking. In eds. Holyoak, K. J. & Morrison, R. G. (2012). *The Oxford Handbook of Thinking and Reasoning.* Oxford, UK: Oxford University Press, 390-412.

Moyers, B. (2014). *Understanding the Propaganda Campaign Against Public Education.* Perspectives. Blog. Retrieved from http://billmoyers.com/2014/03/25.

Murray, K. T., & Murray, B. A. (2010, November 30). Enhancing School Revenue: Combined Reporting and Closing the Door to Corporate Tax Avoidance. *The American School Board Journal,* 36–38.

Patrick, J. J. (1999). The Concept of Citizenship in Education for Democracy. In Charles F. Bahmueller and John J. Patrick (Eds.). *Principles and Practices of Education for Democratic Citizenship: International Perspectives and Projects.* Retrieved from https://eric.ed.gov/?id=434866

PDK. (2017). *Attitudes Toward the Public Schools.* Retrieved from http://www.pdkpoll.org

Petrilli, M., Finn, C., Hentges, C. & Northern, A. M. (2009). "When Private Schools Take Public Dollars: What's the Place of Accountability in School Voucher Programs?" Washington, DC: The Fordham Foundation. Retrieved from https://edexcellence.net/publications/when-private-schools-take.html

Piaget, J. (1952). *The Origins of Intelligence in Children.* New York: International Universities Press.

Poole, M. S., & Van de Ven, A. H. (1989). Using Paradox to Build Management and Organization Theories. *Academy of Management Review, (14)*4, 562–578. doi:10.5465/AMR.1989.4308389

Ravitch, D. (2013). *Reign of Error: The Hoax of the Privatization Movement and the Danger to America's Public Schools.* New York: Alfred A. Knopf.

Ravitch, D. (2018, February 20). Indiana: GOP Legislator Proposes Total Privatization of Muncie School District. *Diane Ravitch's blog.* Retrieved from https://dianeravitch.net/2018/02/20/indiana-gop-legislator-proposes-total-privatization-of-muncie-school-district

Rich, M. (2014, April 25). A Walmart Fortune, Spreading Charter Schools. *The New York Times.* Retrieved from http://nyti.ms/1ldQYu5

Ringold, D. J. (2005). Vulnerability in the Marketplace: Concepts, Caveats, and Possible Solutions. *Journal of Macromarketing,* 25(2), 202–214. doi:10.1177/0276146705281094

Ritchart, R., & Perkins, D. N. (2005). Learning to Think: The Challenges of Teaching Thinking. In Keith J. Holyoak & Robert G. Morrison (Eds.) *The Cambridge Handbook of Thinking and Reasoning.* 775–802. Retrieved from https://pdfs.semanticscholar.org/0e3b/9e4de493894a79f579155c09f0c4f006ac88

Rouse, C. E., & Barrow, L. (2008, August 6). School Vouchers and Student Achievement: Recent Evidence, Remaining Questions. *Annual Review of Economics, 1.* Retrieved from http://www.annualreviews.org

Schmoker, M. J. (2006). *Results Now.* Arlington, VA: Association for Supervision and Curriculum Development.

Schneider, C. (2017, March 26). Verdict still out on vouchers. *The Indianapolis Star.* pp. 1A, 3A–4A.

Seaman, M. (2011). Bloom's Taxonomy: Its Evolution, Revision, and Use in the Field of Education. *Curriculum and Teaching Dialogue, 1&2,* 29–43. Retrieved from https://www.questia.com/library/bloom-s-taxonomy-its-evolution-revision-and-use

Singer, S. (2017, February 18). Top 10 Reasons School Choice Is No Choice. *HuffPost*. Retrieved from https://www.huffingtonpost.com/entry/top-10-reasons-school-choice-is-no-choice_us_58a8d52fe4b0b0e1e0e20be3

Smith, V. (2017, January 22). Vic's Statehouse Notes #270. Retrieved from http://www.icpe-monroecounty.org/blog/vics-statehouse-otes-270-january-22-2017

Sternberg, R. J., & Grigorenko, E. L. (2004). Successful Intelligence in the Classroom. *Theory Into Practice, (43)*4, 274–280. Retrieved from www.tandfonline.com/doi/abs/10.1207/s15430421tip4304_5

Sternberg, R. J., Reznitskaya, A., & Jarvin, L. (2007). Teaching for Wisdom: What Matters Is Not Just What Students Know, but How They Use It. *London Review of Education. (5)*2, 143-158. doi:10.1080/14748460701440830

Stitzlein, S. M. (2017, September 5). How to Define Public Schooling in the Age of Choice? *Education Week*. Retrieved from http://www.edweek.org/ew/articles/2017/09/06/how-to-define-public-schooling-in-the.html

Strauss, V. (2015, August 25). One Alarming Map Shows What Today's School "Reformers" Are Missing. *The Washington Post*. Retrieved from https://www.washingtonpost.com/one-alarming-mapshows-what-todays-school

Thorsen, C., Gustafsson, JE., & Cliffordson, C. (2014). The Influence of Fluid and Crystallized Intelligence on the Development of Knowledge and Skills. *British Journal of Educational Psychology, (84)*4, 556–570. Retrieved from https://www.ncbi.nim.nih.gov/pubmed/24909645

Ujifusa, A. (2016, December 1). See Betsy DeVos' Donations to Senators Who Will Oversee Her Confirmation. *Education Week's blogs*. Retrieved from http://blogs.edweek.org/edweek/campaign-k-12/2016/12/campaign_contributions_betsy_devos_education_secretary.

Ujifusa, A. (2018a, February 12). Trump Seeks to Cut Education Budget by 5 Percent, Expand School Choice Push. *Education Week*. Retrieved from www.blogs.edweek.org/

Ujifusa, A. (2018b, March 23). President Trump Signs Spending Bill That Includes Billions More for Education. *Education Week's Blogs*. Retrieved from http://blogs.edweek.org/edweek/

Ujifusa, A. (2018c, April 10). Military Coalition Tells Congress not to Raid Federal Budget for School Choice. *Education Week's Blogs*. Retrieved from http://blogs.edweek.org/edweek/

Underwood, J., & Mead, J. F. (2012). A Smart ALEC Threatens Public Education. *Phi Delta Kappa International, (93)*6, 51–55. Retrieved from http://www.edweek.org/ew/articles/2012/03/01/kappan_underwood.html?cmp=eml-contshr-shr-desk

Underwood, J. & Mead, J. F. (2012). A Smart ALEC Threatens Public Education. *Kappan. (93)*6. 51–55. Retrieved from www.kappanmagazine.org

USDOE (United States Department of Education). (2000, December). Monitoring School Quality: An Indicators Report. Washington, DC: National Center for Education Statistics. Retrieved from https://nces.ed.gov/pubs2001/2001030

US Securities and Exchange Commission (n.d.) *An Introduction to 529 Plans*. Retrieved from https://www.sec.gov/reportspubs/.

Walsh, M. (2017, October 12). "Backpack Full of Cash" Documentary Fuels Controversy Over School Choice. *Education Week*. Retrieved from http://blogs.edweek.org/edweek/education_and_the_media/2017/10/back-pack_full_of_cash_film_packs_controversy_over_portrayal_of_school_choice

Wermund, B. (2016, December 2). Vouchers Have Been a Tough Sell When Put to a Vote. *Morning Education POLITICO*. Retrieved from www.politico.com/tipsheets/morning-education/2016/12/vouchers-have-been-a-tough-sell-when-put-to-a-vote-219907

Westervelt, E. (2016, December 7). Trump's Pick For Education: A Free Market Approach to School Choice. *All Things Considered: NPR*. Retrieved from www.npr.org/sections/ed/2016/12/07504696506/trumps-pick-for-education-a-free-market-approach-to-school-choice

Winstead, L. (2004). Increasing Academic Motivation and Cognition in Reading, Writing, and Mathematics: Meaning-Making Strategies. *Educational Research Quarterly, (28)*2, 29–47. Retrieved from https://eric.ed.gov/?id=EJ718129

Wong, H. (nd). *Major Concepts Covered By Harry K. Wong*. Retrieved from http://thebusyeducator.com/harry=wong.htm

Wong, K. K. & Shen, F. X. (2006). Charter Law and Charter Outcomes: Re-Examining the Charter School Marketplace. Prepared for the National Conference on Charter School Research at Vanderbilt University, September 29, 2006. National Center on School Choice. Retrieved from https://eric.ed.gov/?id=ED509549

Yeh, S. S. (2010). The Cost Effectiveness of 22 Approaches for Raising Student Achievement. *Journal of Education Finance, (36)*1, 38–75. Retrieved from https://eric.ed.gov/?id=EJ893876

Zernike, K. (2016, December 12). How Trump's Education Nominee Bent Detroit to Her Will on Charter Schools. *The New York Times*. Retrieved from http://nyti.ms/2gzJXds

Index

ALEC. *See* American Legislative Exchange Council
American Legislative Exchange Council (ALEC), 45, 46, 49, 72, 100, 116, 120, 122

Bloom, Benjamin, 20, 21, 23, 38; taxonomy, 24

charter schools, 97, 103
choice education, 6, 94
competition, 11

democracy, 79, 82, 83, 88, 115, 126
DeVos, Betsy, 47
Dewey, John, 5
diversity, 89

e pluribus unum, 81
education: primary purpose of, 5, 18, 27, 57, 58, 84, 87
efficiency, 11

free market schooling, 6, 49, 52, 62, 98, 116; context of, 13, 51, 56; federal funding for, 111; marketplace, 12; state funding for, 67; theory of, 7, 9, 42, 54, 73, 74, 88, 94, 98
function, 36, 38, 60, 126

GPPS. *See* Guided Professional Practice Selections
Guided Professional Practice Selections (GPPS), 20, 36, 38, 60

habits of mind, 20, 21, 30, 36
Hunter, Madeline, 36

information processing, 91, 92, 97
instruction, 34; examples of, 34, 36

instructional mapping, 60

Kegan, Robert, 26, 60
Kohlberg, Lawrence, 27

Marjory Stoneman Douglas High School, 85, 86
market failure, 10, 11, 13
mechanisms, 10, 12, 42, 54, 106
model-for, 7, 17
model-of, 7
morphogenesis, theory of, 58, 59, 64
my-side bias, 13, 83, 91, 104

points of practice, 18, 22, 23; adopting a definition of learning, 31; adopting a definition of thinking, 29; cognitive agency, 32, 57, 61, 118; meaning making, 26, 60; natural thinking, 25, 35; responsive cognition, 32, 61, 84, 126
policy bubble, 53, 54, 56
policy-makers, 53, 55, 63, 64, 76
privatization, 14, 51, 55, 56, 76, 95, 99, 103, 105, 117
professional practice, 18, 19, 22, 23, 27, 59, 85, 88
public education, traditional, 15, 27, 41, 52, 62, 81, 90, 99, 121, 124; funding of, 68
public good, 10, 79, 80, 82, 92; definition of, 89

ROI. *See* Return on Investment
RTS. *See* Return to Students
Return on Investment (ROI), 9, 48, 109, 110
Return to Students (RTS), 9, 74, 111

segregation, 101, 105, 109, 117

Shanker, Albert, 97
social justice, 126
special education, 77
standardized testing, 54
students, 105, 107, 111; achievement, 102; learning style, 33
successful intelligence, 87

tax credits, 69
thinking-scapes, 32, 35

transformative learning theory, 35

virtual schools, 106, 107
vouchers, 52, 68, 99, 101, 102, 103, 117
Vygotsky, Lev, 7, 91

wisdom, 85, 86

zone of proximal development, 7

About the Authors

Dr. Jeff Swensson, PhD, served for forty-five years as an educator in K–16 public education. His extensive experience in diverse school communities as a teacher, school leader, district leader, and assistant professor give him a perspective enriched by innumerable opportunities for meaningful conversations, instructional leadership, and continuous professional improvement. His scholar/practitioner interests include school leadership, quality school practices, and traditional public education. He is the author of peer-reviewed articles, a newspaper column, and thank-you notes to countless colleagues whose expertise makes a profound difference for students.

Dr. John Ellis, PhD, served public education across Indiana as a teacher, assistant principal, principal, assistant superintendent, superintendent, and executive director of the Indiana Association of Public School Superintendents for more than forty-three years. He graduated from Ball State University with a BA, a Master's, and EdS in Education before earning his PhD from Indiana State University. As a superintendent he wrote a weekly newspaper education column. He is the author and co-author of published peer-reviewed articles focusing primarily on school finance, the school superintendency, and the impact of politics on education.

Dr. Michael Shaffer, EdD, is an assistant professor of educational leadership at Ball State University. He currently teaches politics, school finance, school facilities, human resources, and the central office administration. Shaffer has been very involved in writing in support of traditional public education. He has also traveled extensively speaking on the topic of literacy and the process of getting boys to read. Prior to coming full time to Ball State, Shaffer served in a number of schools and school districts, both public and private, as a principal at all levels and as an assistant superintendent.

www.ingramcontent.com/pod-product-compliance
Lightning Source LLC
Chambersburg PA
CBHW020747230426
43665CB00009B/531